50
THINGS YOU SHOULD KNOW ABOUT

PREHISTORIC BRITAIN

by Clare Hibbert

Consultant: Dr Benjamin Roberts,
Durham University
Illustrators: Laszlo Veres, Sam Weston,
Philip Schwartzberg (maps)
Project Editor: Carly Madden
Editorial Director: Victoria Garrard
Art Director: Laura Roberts-Jensen
Associate Publisher: Maxime Boucknooghe
Publisher: Zeta Jones

**Designed, edited and picture-researched
by:** Starry Dog Books Ltd

Copyright © QED Publishing 2015

First published in the UK in 2015 by
QED Publishing
Part of The Quarto Group
The Old Brewery, 6 Blundell Street,
London, N7 9BH

www.qed-publishing.co.uk

A catalogue record for this book is available from
the British Library.

ISBN 978 1 78493 305 0

Printed in China

Words in **bold** are explained
in the Glossary on page 78.

CONTENTS

INTRODUCTION

Prehistory means the time before history was written down. It can refer to the whole span of time on Earth before writing, including the billions of years before there was human life on this planet! But for most historians, 'prehistory' means human history before written records.

About 140 to 100 mya, what is now southern Britain was swampy woodland, home to dinosaurs such as Iguanodon, Polacanthus and Baryonyx.

Iguanodon

Polacanthus

Baryonyx

BRITAIN BEFORE PEOPLE

The time from 230 to 65 million years ago (mya) was the age of the dinosaurs. The oldest dinosaur remains found in Britain belong to *Thecodontosaurus*, which lived 210 mya. At that time, the British Isles didn't exist as separate islands – they were part of the one huge area of land called Pangaea.

LAND MASSES

At the start of the dinosaur age (230 mya), all the land was clumped into one giant continent, called Pangaea. By 160 mya, Pangaea had broken apart into two land masses, Laurasia and Gondwana. The land slowly broke apart to form the continents. Britain had separated from mainland Europe by 6000 BCE.

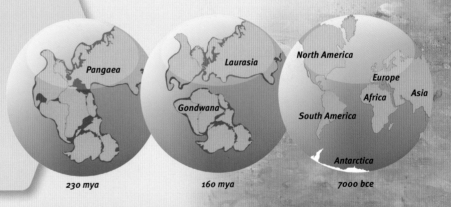

Pangaea

230 mya

Laurasia

Gondwana

160 mya

North America

Europe

Africa

Asia

South America

Antarctica

7000 bce

KEY EVENTS

c. 3.3 mya
The Old Stone Age begins, as early humans in Africa begin to use simple stone tools.

c. 900,000 ya
The earliest humans arrive in Britain. They are **hunter-gatherers**.

c. 11,500 ya
In Britain, the Old Stone Age ends about the time of the last **Ice Age**. The Middle Stone Age begins.

c. 6000 ya (4000 BCE)
The New Stone Age begins in Britain. People begin to live as farmers instead of hunter-gatherers.

▼ Early hunter-gatherers worked together to bring down rhino and other large animals. They butchered their kills quickly before hungry lions moved in!

PREHISTORIC BRITAIN

The first humans in prehistoric Britain arrived about 900,000 years ago (ya). These people were hunter-gatherers, who lived simple lives scavenging or hunting, picking berries and nuts to eat, and sleeping in caves or other simple shelters. Gradually, over hundreds of thousands of years, humans learnt how to grow crops and live more ordered lives in villages and towns. The prehistoric period in Britain ended about 43 BCE, when the **Romans** arrived and began to conquer the land.

THREE AGES

There were three main periods of prehistory in Britain: the Stone Age, the Bronze Age and the Iron Age. The names of these periods are based on the types of tools that people were using at the time.

▶ A human species called Homo heidelbergensis arrived in Britain about 500,000 ya. He made simple stone tools.

c. **2500** BCE
The Copper Age begins in Britain when people learn to shape copper. Soon they can work tin and gold, too.

c. **2200** BCE
People in Britain learn how to make things from bronze. The Bronze Age begins.

c. **1000** BCE
People in Britain learn how to make things from iron. The Iron Age begins about 200 years later.

c. **43** BCE
The Iron Age ends. The Romans invade Britain and written history begins.

THE OLD STONE AGE

1

The Stone Age is the time when early people used stone tools. **Archaeologists** divide it into three shorter periods. The first period, the Old Stone Age (or **Palaeolithic**), began at least 3.3 million years ago, and lasted until about the end of the Ice Age, roughly 11,500 years ago.

▶ Homo sapiens *(modern humans) evolved about 200,000 years ago. We spread out of Africa about 65,000 years ago, arriving in Britain about 40,000 years ago.*

OUT OF AFRICA

The first humans lived in Africa about seven million years ago. They had gradually developed, or evolved, from ape-like ancestors. Today there is only one human species, *Homo sapiens*, but during our evolution there have been more than 20 different species!

FLINT TOOLS

The oldest stone tools found in Britain are flint handaxes. They were discovered at Happisburgh in Norfolk and are about 900,000 years old.

15,000 ya

NORTH AMERICA

1400 ya

12,000 ya

SOUTH AMERICA

MAP KEY

▬ *Migration routes of* Homo sapiens

KEY EVENTS

c. 900,000 ya	*c.* 650,000 ya	*c.* 500,000 ya	*c.* 400,000 ya	*c.* 300,000 ya
Hunter-gathering *Homo erectus* (human) arrives in Britain. He uses simple stone tools.	An ice age drives away *Homo erectus*.	Britain enters a warm time between icy periods. *Homo heidelbergensis* arrives (see page 5).	Britain is covered with ice. People and animals leave to find warmer places.	People in Britain find a new way of making sharper stone tools.

THE STORY OF EVOLUTION

Evolution is the gradual change that happens to species over time. If an animal is suited to its surroundings, it is more likely to survive and have babies, and pass on its own characteristics to its offspring. In this way, species very gradually change to be better suited to their environment.

MISSING LINK?

People slowly accepted the idea of evolution, but there were not many fossils of early humans. The hunt was on to find the missing link between apes and humans. In 1912, a man named Charles Dawson showed off a skull that he said he had dug up at Piltdown in Sussex. It seemed human but its jaw was like an ape's. Experts were amazed and said the fossil was 500,000 years old! However, in 1953, Piltdown Man was shown to be a fake.

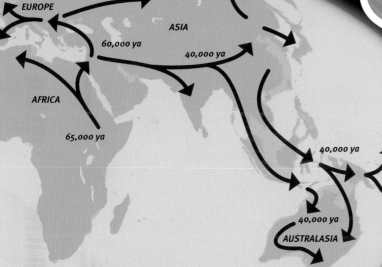

25,000 ya

40,000 ya
EUROPE

ASIA

60,000 ya

40,000 ya

AFRICA

65,000 ya

40,000 ya

40,000 ya
AUSTRALASIA

▲ *The Piltdown skull was from a modern human, but the jaw and teeth were probably from an orang-utan.*

Australopithecus
(3–2 mya)

Homo habilis
(2.4–1.5 mya)

Homo erectus
(1.8 mya–70,000 ya)

Homo neanderthalensis
300,000–250,000 ya–40,000 ya

Homo sapiens
(200,000 ya to the present)

▶ Australopithecus *was one of the earliest human species. Its descendents include* Homo habilis, Homo erectus, Homo neanderthalensis *and us,* Homo sapiens.

c. 200,000 ya	*c.* 65,000 ya	*c.* 60,000 ya	*c.* 40,000 ya	*c.* 13,000 ya
People begin to make tools in different shapes, suitable for different jobs.	Modern humans (*Homo sapiens*) leave Africa and settle across Europe and the Middle East.	Neanderthal humans (*Homo neanderthalensis*) arrive in Britain.	*Homo sapiens* arrive in Britain and Neanderthals disappear.	People decorate the cave walls at Creswell Crags (see page 12).

2 Ice ages

During the Old Stone Age, the climate warmed up and cooled down many times. In the cold (glacial) periods, ice sheets and **glaciers** covered much of the planet. Together, the colder and warmer periods were part of much longer time spans called ice ages.

CLIMATE CHANGE AND PEOPLE

The changing climate affected where people could hunt. In southern Britain, winters were bleak and the land was frozen, but in spring it thawed briefly and grass grew. This meant animals could graze. People hunted the animals for their meat using simple stone tools and weapons.

THE FIVE MAJOR ICE AGES

Since the Earth formed about 4.6 billion years ago, it has had five major ice ages.

Huronian
2.4–2.1 billion years ago

Cryogenian
850–630 mya

Andean-Saharan
460–430 mya

Karoo
360–260 mya

Quarternary
2.58 mya to present

▼ *The last cold period in Britain lasted from 18,000 to 16,000 years ago. Then the ice began to retreat.*

▲ *A reindeer grazes on tundra – the type of landscape Britain had during the Ice Age.*

THE ICE AGE

The last cold period was at its coldest 18,000 years ago. It is often called the Ice Age (with capital letters). Temperatures were 15 to 20 degrees lower than they are today. There was less rainfall, because much of the world's water was ice.

Ice Age animals

The Ice Age is famous for its giant animals. During the cold periods, Britain was home to huge mammoths and woolly rhinos. In warmer times, lions, rhinos, hippos and elephants roamed the woods and grasslands.

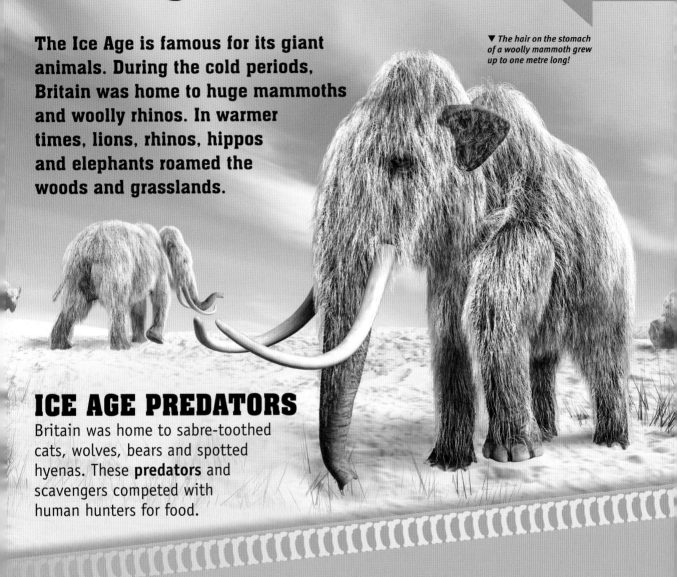

▼ *The hair on the stomach of a woolly mammoth grew up to one metre long!*

ICE AGE PREDATORS

Britain was home to sabre-toothed cats, wolves, bears and spotted hyenas. These **predators** and scavengers competed with human hunters for food.

WOOLLY RHINO

- Lived in Britain 190,000–36,000 years ago.
- Adult males weighed about 3 tonnes.
- Small ears and tail meant less risk of frostbite.
- Two horns, about 60 centimetres and 15 centimetres long.
- Lifespan was more than 30 years.

WOOLLY MAMMOTH

- Lived in Britain 190,000–14,000 years ago.
- Adult males weighed up to 6 tonnes.
- Small ears and tail meant less risk of frostbite.
- Pair of tusks up to 4.2 metres long.
- Lifespan was up to 60 years.

Early homes

4

Hunter-gatherers in the Old Stone Age moved from place to place. Most of them did not build permanent homes. Instead, they put up rough shelters to protect themselves from the wind and rain.

KEEPING WARM

Archaeologists have found hearths in caves used by early people, but they haven't found any tools for starting fires, such as **fire drills**. It is most likely that people in the Old Stone Age did not know how to start fires, but they could keep fire alight if they found it, for example after a lightning strike.

▲ People used smouldering branches found after lightning strikes to light fires in their shelters.

▲ Early people are sometimes known as 'cave people' but there were very few caves in prehistoric Britain. Most people lived in makeshift shelters.

BONE HOUSES

At a few Old Stone Age sites, the remains of more permanent homes have been found. Some were made of stone or wood, and others were built from mammoth bones! The best-preserved mammoth bone settlement is at Mezhirich in Ukraine. The huts there were built 14,000 to 15,000 years ago.

▲ Each of the four bone huts found at Mezhirich was big enough for three families to share.

Sculptures and carvings

People in the Old Stone Age did not spend all their time just trying to survive. They were also creative and had imaginations. We know this because of the amazing art they made, such as sculptures and carvings of animals and people, and cave paintings (see pages 12–13). We also know they had musical instruments.

MAKING MUSIC

People played music on drums made from animal skins and flutes carved from bones. They probably sang, too! Some of the oldest bone flutes date from 35,000 to 40,000 years ago and were found in Hohle Fels, an Old Stone Age cave in Germany. An even older bear-bone flute has been found in Slovenia.

▼ Artists made small objects that they could take with them. This horse, found in Vogelherd Cave, Germany, is only 4.8 centimetres long.

▲ Some of the flutes found in Hohle Fels cave were carved from mammoth bone, but one was made of vulture bone.

ART MATERIALS

Ice Age artists used simple flint knives to carve mammoth ivory (tusk), reindeer antler, bone and stone. They sometimes added colour by making paint from an earthy powder, or pigment, called red ochre. The objects they made were small enough to be carried from camp to camp.

▲ This small sculpture of a mammoth was made about 35,000 years ago from ivory.

Cave art

Cave paintings are the most famous examples of Old Stone Age art. Europe has some spectacular prehistoric caves. Most cave art features the animals that people hunted for food – horses, bison, aurochs (wild cattle), ibex, reindeer, red deer and musk oxen.

Eye

Body of bird

Curved beak

▲ The carvings at Creswell Crags in Derbyshire are the most northern examples of cave art in Europe.

CAVE ART IN BRITAIN

In 2003, archaeologists discovered carvings on the walls of limestone caves at Creswell Crags in Derbyshire, England – the first known cave art in Britain. The caves contain more than 80 wall engravings of stags, bison, birds and people, all made more than 13,000 years ago.

WORLDWIDE

France and Spain have some of Europe's most famous prehistoric cave art. There are examples in Africa, Australia, parts of Asia and the Americas, too.

A reindeer carved at Cathole Cave in Wales dates back at least 14,000 years.

EARLIEST ART

The oldest-known cave paintings – animals and hands at Maros on Sulawesi, Indonesia – date from about 40,000 years ago.

▶ Prehistoric artists used fine hollow bones to spray paint around their hands to make handprints.

◀ *Chauvet Cave in southern France has hundreds of paintings, some made more than 30,000 years ago. Here, you can see four horses, three bulls and a rhinoceros.*

COLOURS

Cave artists used only a few colours – black, red ochre and yellow ochre. Black came from a mineral called manganese or from charcoal (burnt sticks). Red and yellow ochre also came from minerals found in soft rocks. The rocks were ground into powder, which was mixed with water to make a sticky paint.

▲ This reconstruction shows an artist in the Cave of Altimira, Spain. He is using red ochre to paint a bison.

▶ Red ochre

7 The Neanderthals

The Neanderthals are the most famous of all the early human species. They lived across **Eurasia** for more than 200,000 years (before modern humans arrived). Their short, stocky bodies were perfectly adapted to cold climates.

Ape   Neanderthal   Modern human

CLOSE COUSINS

DNA is the special chemical found in every cell of every living thing. It carries tens of thousands of instructions that decide what that living thing is like. In 2010, scientists studied the DNA of a Neanderthal. More than 99 per cent of his DNA was exactly the same as the DNA of modern humans. This means that modern humans and Neanderthals have a common ancestor who lived in Africa about 500,000 years ago.

▲ Archaeologists have found Neanderthal graves. These suggest that Neanderthals had rituals and spiritual beliefs.

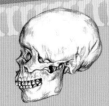

HOMO NEANDERTHALENSIS

- Appeared in Eurasia 300,000–250,000 ya.
- In Britain 60,000–40,000 ya.
- Average brain size 1600 cubic centimetres.
- Height up to 1.68 metres.
- Ridged brow; low, sloping forehead.

HOMO SAPIENS

- Appeared in Africa 200,000 ya.
- In Britain 40,000 ya–present.
- Average brain size 1400 cubic centimetres.
- Height up to 1.85 metres.
- Small brow ridge; high, flat forehead.

Neanderthals are named after the Neander valley in Germany.

HUNTING AND TECHNOLOGY

Experts think that Neanderthals mostly ate meat and not much else. Often they took it from the dead bodies of animals that had been killed by predators, but sometimes they hunted animals themselves. The stone handaxes that Neanderthals used were better than those made by earlier humans because, by this time, people had learnt how to make different-shaped flint flakes.

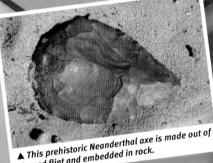

▲ This prehistoric Neanderthal axe is made out of shaped flint and embedded in rock.

▶ Reconstruction of a Neanderthal face. It is possible that Neanderthals had spoken language.

END OF THE NEANDERTHALS

Neanderthals died out in Britain at about the same time that modern humans arrived. Another cold period was just beginning, so there was less food to go around. Perhaps modern humans were better at planning their hunts and the Neanderthals could not compete.

▲ Gorham's Cave on Gibraltar is one of the last-known Neanderthal sites. It was lived in until about 28,000 years ago.

THE MIDDLE STONE AGE

8

The Middle Stone Age (**Mesolithic**) lasted from the end of the Ice Age, about **11,500** years ago, until **6000** years ago. People still lived by hunting and gathering, but they were more settled. They built camps, which they returned to year after year, and they even knew how to make fire!

▲ Middle Stone Age re-enactors make fire using a bow drill. The bow turned the wooden drill very fast, creating enough heat to start a fire.

LOOKING FOR CLUES

All sorts of things help archaeologists to build up a picture of life long ago. Even footprints tell a story. At low tide, you can see Middle Stone Age footprints in the estuary at Goldcliff East, south Wales. They were pressed into clay and later hardened into fossils. One set belongs to a group made up of two adults, a child aged 10 or 11 who was running around, and a younger child aged three or four.

▲ The footprints at Goldcliff East include 35 human prints, plus prints from seabirds and a deer.

KEY EVENTS

c. 11,500 ya	*c.* 10,700–10,350 ya	*c.* 9600 ya	*c.* 9500 ya
The Ice Age ends and Britain warms up.	People live at Star Carr in Yorkshire (see pages 22–23).	Middle Stone Age people build the Howick House in Northumberland.	A carved wooden totem, now known as the Shigir idol, is made in the Urals, Russia (see page 19).

ISLAND BRITAIN

At the start of the Middle Stone Age, Britain was still connected to mainland Europe by a low-lying area of land called Doggerland. Around 6200 BCE, this was flooded, probably by a tidal wave. A tiny island (Dogger Island) remained but soon it, too, was submerged under the North Sea. Britain became an island.

NORWAY

DOGGERLAND

SCOTLAND

DENMARK

Howick House ●

Star Carr ●

IRELAND

DOGGERLAND

WALES

ENGLAND

Goldcliff East ●

● Gough's Cave

MAP KEY

Land above sea level

	16,000 bce
	8000 bce
	7000 bce
	Land area today

FRANCE

---

c. 9000 ya
Cheddar Man is living in Gough's Cave, Cheddar Gorge, Somerset (see page 21).

c. 8000 ya
Melting glaciers create the English Channel and North Sea. Britain becomes an island.

Humans and animals leave footprints that fossilise in the silty mud at Goldcliff East, south Wales.

c. 6000 ya
People bury their dead with **grave goods**, including antlers and beads, at Vedbaek in Denmark.

Middle Stone Age tools

During the Middle Stone Age, people began to make a new type of tool called a microlith. This was a small blade used to slice, saw or scrape. It was made by snapping a piece of flint and flaking off little bits of stone to make notches or grooves. Microliths were sometimes attached to handles to make all sorts of useful weapons and tools.

BOWS AND ARROWS

Bows and arrows first appeared in the later part of the Old Stone Age and became more widespread in the Middle Stone Age. Hunters fixed microliths into wooden shafts and fired them from wooden bows. Not many have survived.

◄ People used birch resin (sticky tree sap) to attach microliths to handles of bone, antler or wood.

FLINT-KNAPPING

Knapping means hitting stone to create flakes or chips.

- Take a large piece of flint called a core.

- Strike the flint near the edge with a round pebble, called a hammerstone, to flake off thin pieces of stone.

- Use the flakes to make scrapers and cutters.

► A flint knapper at work on a piece of flint.

BUILDING WITH WOOD

People living along coasts or by rivers used their axes to hollow out tree trunks and make dugout canoes. Wood was also a useful building material. At Middle Stone Age sites across Britain and Ireland, archaeologists have found holes that held timber posts for buildings.

Learning to use wood

Another new tool appeared in the Middle Stone Age – the tranchet axe. This was made by working a piece of flint into an oval shape, then removing a large flake from one end to create a cutting edge. Attached to a handle, this axe allowed people to practise carpentry for the first time.

▶ Reconstruction of the Middle Stone Age house at Howick, Northumberland. The original house was lived in on-and-off for at least 100 years.

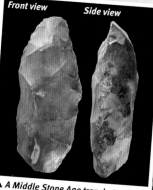
Front view   Side view

▲ A Middle Stone Age tranchet axe made of flint.

▲ The Shigir idol is several metres tall. It has a carved head.

WOODEN ARTEFACTS

Only a few wooden objects survive from the Middle Stone Age. At Shigir in Russia's Ural Mountains, archaeologists found a wooden idol (an object that could represent a god, spirit or ancestor). It was preserved in a **peat bog**.

Animals in the Middle Stone Age

Many large animals roamed Britain in the Middle Stone Age. There were deer and wild boar, moose, bears and aurochs. We know that people hunted and ate these animals because their bones were preserved in fossilized 'rubbish heaps'. Hunter-gatherers also caught smaller animals, such as wild cats, beavers, birds, fish and shellfish.

▶ *Middle Stone Age people hunted red deer, like this one, and roe deer, which are smaller and grey-brown.*

MAN'S BEST FRIEND

Hunters during the Middle Stone Age had a very useful hunting companion – the dog. It had been **domesticated**, or tamed, during the Late Old Stone Age, either from a grey wolf or a wolf-like animal. In return for its help hunting, the dog received a share of the feast. It soon had a special place in people's lives.

▲ *The dog was probably domesticated from the grey wolf.*

Cheddar Man

The oldest complete human skeleton found in Britain belongs to Cheddar Man, a hunter-gatherer who lived more than 9000 years ago. His remains were discovered in Gough's Cave in Cheddar Gorge, Somerset. DNA taken from the bones matches the DNA of some people who still live in Cheddar – they are Cheddar Man's direct descendants!

HOW DID CHEDDAR MAN DIE?

Cheddar Man has a hole in his skull, and there are unexplained cuts in the other skulls and bones found in the cave. Perhaps these people were **sacrifices** to the gods.

▲ Cheddar Man's skeleton. He was about 23 years old when he died.

▲ Gough's Cave was a shelter for early people. There was good hunting nearby and a freshwater spring.

HORSE HUNTERS

There are horse bones in Gough's Cave that date back 14,700 years. People living in the cave during the Old Stone Age hunted wild horses for meat. They made the herd of horses panic and run, guiding them towards the edge of a cliff so that they fell to their deaths.

Star Carr

The Star Carr camp was inhabited for about 300 years.

Star Carr in North Yorkshire is Britain's most important Middle Stone Age site. Today, the area is covered with fields, but about 11,000 years ago there was a large lake there, with settlements dotted around it. Star Carr was one of those settlements.

VIKING NAME

The name Star Carr was probably given to the site long after people first settled there, when Vikings from Scandinavia arrived in the area. The Danish words *star kjaer* mean 'sedge fen' – fen is wetland and sedge is a wetland grass.

AN EPIC DISCOVERY

Amateur archaeologist John Moore discovered Star Carr in 1948. He found flints and horse bones preserved in the peat. Moore convinced Grahame Clark of Cambridge University to **excavate**. Clark's team discovered thousands of objects – bone and antler artefacts, butchered remains of animals, shale beads and wooden platforms.

▲ *Archaeologists excavating the site at Star Carr, 1949–1951.*

▼ *The huts at Star Carr were built next to a lake.*

EVERYDAY LIFE

The Star Carr camp was a busy centre of industry. People made tools from flint brought from 20 kilometres away. They also made objects from bone, antler and wood. They hunted in the surrounding woodlands and fished in the lake. No boats have been found yet, but a wooden boat paddle has been excavated.

▼ Twenty-one red deer skull masks like this one have been found at Star Carr.

The most spectacular artefacts from Star Carr are frontlets (masks) made from the skulls of red deer. Their insides were smoothed and the antlers were hollowed out to make them lighter. The masks were probably worn for special rituals or dances.

▲ This skeleton of a woman was found at a Middle Stone Age site in Brittany, France. She was buried wearing a shell necklace.

READING THE SIGNS

The masks at Star Carr suggest that the people had ceremonies and beliefs. Elsewhere, archaeologists have found Middle Stone Age graves where people were buried with precious objects. Perhaps these grave goods were for the dead to use in the afterlife.

THE NEW STONE AGE

The **Neolithic**, or New Stone Age, began about **6000 years ago** (about **4000 BCE**). People at this time slowly began to switch from hunting and gathering food to farming. They began to build more permanent settlements, and they also put up amazing stone monuments (megaliths) that are still standing. The New Stone Age lasted until people discovered how to work metal. In Britain, that happened about **2500 BCE**.

▲ The Ancient Egyptians were one of the first peoples to learn to farm. Here, an Egyptian priest is offering up wheat to the sun god, Horus.

BCE

When we talk about specific dates in prehistory, we use the letters BCE after the date. These stand for 'Before the Common Era'. They refer to the years before the believed birth of Jesus, about 2000 years ago. So, 4000 BCE is about 6000 years ago.

THE BIRTH OF FARMING

Farming began about 11,500 years ago in Mesopotamia (ancient Iraq). The earliest farmers grew wild species of wheat and barley. Gradually, over time, farmers learned to improve their crops by always choosing the fattest grains to sow for their next harvest. They bred better animals in the same way, selecting those that produced the most milk or the best meat. Over thousands of years, farming skills spread west and eventually arrived in Britain.

KEY EVENTS

c. 4000 BCE
Farming arrives in Britain (see page 26). People begin to make pottery (see page 32).

c. 3800 BCE
The Sweet Track is built in what is now Somerset (see page 27).

c. 3300 BCE
Ötzi the Iceman is alive (see page 33). The Carnac stones are erected in France (see pages 25 and 37).

c. 3200 BCE
The mound at Newgrange in County Meath, Ireland, is built (see page 36).

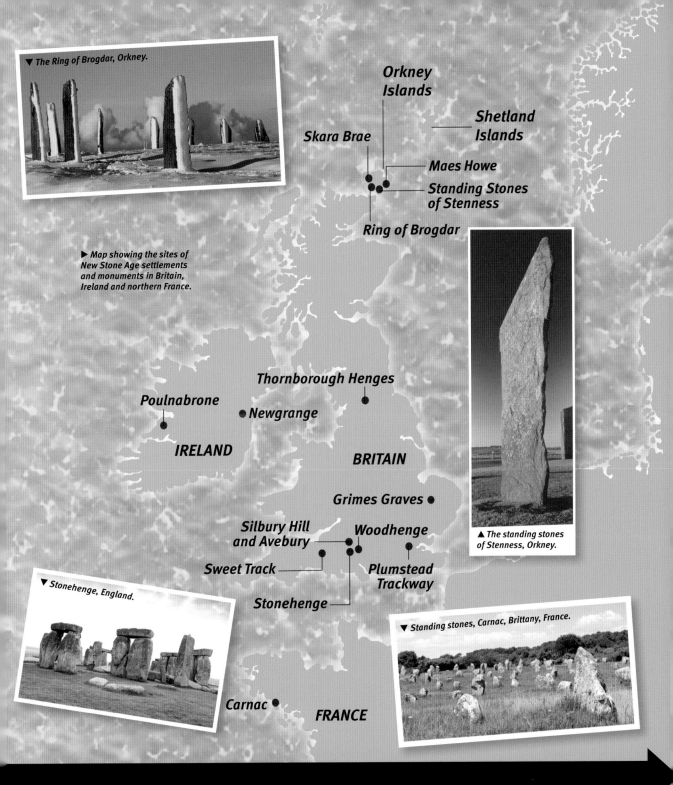

▼ The Ring of Brogdar, Orkney.

Orkney Islands

Shetland Islands

Skara Brae

Maes Howe

Standing Stones of Stenness

▶ Map showing the sites of New Stone Age settlements and monuments in Britain, Ireland and northern France.

Ring of Brogdar

Thornborough Henges

Poulnabrone

● Newgrange

IRELAND

BRITAIN

▲ The standing stones of Stenness, Orkney.

Grimes Graves ●

Silbury Hill and Avebury

Woodhenge

Sweet Track

Plumstead Trackway

▼ Stonehenge, England.

Stonehenge

▼ Standing stones, Carnac, Brittany, France.

Carnac ●

FRANCE

c. **3200 to 2500** BCE
People build and inhabit the village of Skara Brae on Orkney (see pages 28–29).

c. **3000 to 1000** BCE
People mine flint at Grimes Graves (see pages 30–31).

c. **2500** BCE
Silbury Hill is constructed (see page 35).

c. **2300** BCE
Stonehenge's stone circles and avenue are complete (see pages 38–39).

25

The first farmers

Farming reached Europe from the Middle East about 8000 BCE, and arrived in Britain about 4000 BCE. People raised sheep, goats, cattle and pigs for their milk, meat, wool and leather. They also grew crops such as barley, wheat and **pulses**.

SLOW AND STEADY

People did not stop hunting and gathering straight away. They hunted wild animals as well as raising livestock, and they still gathered nuts, seeds and berries. People began to eat dairy products, too, such as cheese and yoghurt.

NEW TOOLS AND TECHNOLOGY

Farming demanded new tools. People needed to clear woodland to make space to graze their animals and grow their crops. They used polished stone axes, which they could sharpen on stone grinders. They also had curved blades (sickles) for harvesting grain. Grinding stones, called quern stones, were used for grinding wheat into flour.

▼ *A New Stone Age sickle, used for cutting wheat and barley.*

▼ *Sheep were kept for meat and wool. They were brought from Europe in dugout boats (see page 27), along with cattle and goats.*

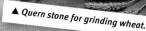

▲ *Quern stone for grinding wheat.*

26

Getting around

New Stone Age people did not have carts, wheeled vehicles or horses to ride. When they travelled, they went on foot. Their ancient paths are called trackways. Sometimes people had to cross marshy ground, so they built raised trackways from wood to make moving around easier.

TRAVEL BY BOAT

When people travelled over water, they used dugout canoes. Unfortunately, because these were made of wood, few have survived – and in Britain no New Stone Age boats have been found.

OLDEST TRACK

The oldest-known timber trackway in northern Europe is 6000 years old. It was discovered in 2009 in Plumstead, southeast London, under five metres of peat.

▲ Construction workers found the Plumstead trackway.

SWEET TRACK

Archaeologists have found the remains of timber trackways that date from New Stone Age times. One of the earliest is the Sweet Track in Somerset. It was built about 3800 BCE on the site of an even older structure, and was made from split trunks of oak.

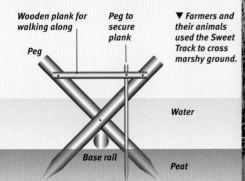

Wooden plank for walking along

Peg to secure plank

▼ Farmers and their animals used the Sweet Track to cross marshy ground.

Peg

Water

Base rail

Peat

◄ A reconstruction of the Sweet Track, which covered a distance of almost two kilometres.

Under the Sweet Track is the Post Track, built 30 years earlier.

New Stone Age village:
Skara Brae

On the Orkney Islands, off northeast Scotland, you can see the remains of Skara Brae – Europe's best-preserved New Stone Age village. The site was dramatically revealed in 1850 by a great storm. It was lived in about 5000 years ago, and has eight houses, linked by stone passages. Even some items of furniture have survived!

All the houses at Skara Brae have just one room, with areas for cooking, sleeping and storage.

BUILT ON RUBBISH

People lived at Skara Brae for about 700 years. The first houses date to about 3000 BCE. The later, larger buildings were built partly underground, dug into the midden (rubbish heap) produced by the earlier inhabitants. The rubbish had turned into a clay-like material that helped to weatherproof the homes.

Little alcoves in the walls were used for storage.

This stone box bed would have been packed with soft bracken and covered with animal skins.

FEEDING THE VILLAGE

. . . .

The people at Skara Brae kept cattle, pigs and sheep or goats, and grew barley and wheat. They caught fish, such as cod and saithe, from the sea. There is whalebone at the site, too, but it probably came from beached whales – no tools suitable for killing whales have been found.

CLOTHING

No clothes survive at Skara Brae. Archaeologists think people wore furs and skins, because they haven't found tools for spinning or weaving, but they have found bone pins. People probably decorated their clothes with bone beads.

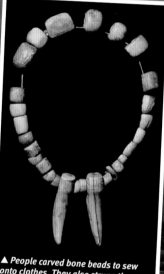

▲ *People carved bone beads to sew onto clothes. They also strung them together to wear as necklaces.*

The stone dresser was probably used to show off prized possessions.

Small stone tanks set into the ground were used for preparing fish bait.

A fire was lit in the hearth for cooking and to heat the house.

THE WORKSHOP

One building at Skara Brae is free-standing instead of being partly buried in the midden. Its floor is covered with fragments of chert, a flint-like stone. Experts think it was a workshop where people made tools.

Flint mining

To make the best stone axes and other tools, New Stone Age people needed good-quality stone. In places that had good flint, people dug mines. They were able to trade with people from other communities, swapping their flint for other useful goods.

▼ *Grimes Graves mineshaft*

GRIMES GRAVES

The largest-known flint mine in Britain during the New Stone Age was Grimes Graves in Norfolk. More than 400 shafts were dug down into the chalk there. The biggest are more than 14 metres deep and 12 metres across – they would have taken 20 men about five months to dig.

SACRED SPACES

Mines were dangerous places. If walls caved in, the men below had little hope of escape. Miners prayed to the gods to keep them safe. Some mines had a special shaft that was used as a shrine for offerings.

Chalk 'goddess' from Grimes Graves

BUILDING AND FILLING IN

Wooden platforms and ladders supported the miners as they dug down to the flint. They piled up the spoil (dug-out material) around the mouth of the shaft. Once they had extracted all the flint from a shaft, they used the spoil to fill it in.

▼ *This cutaway artwork shows what Grimes Graves may have looked like in New Stone Age times.*

Workers bundled the flint into animal skins to carry it to the surface.

Miners at the base of the shaft excavated the nodules or lumps of flint.

▲ *Lumps in the landscape at Grimes Graves show where the shafts were filled in again.*

MINING TOOLS

Miners used picks made from antlers to extract the flint. At Grimes Graves, there was probably a red deer 'farm', with deer that gave the miners antler picks and venison meat. Wooden shovels or the shoulder-blade bones of oxen were used to pile up the spoil.

◀ *Archaeologists have found an average of more than 140 antler picks in each shaft they have excavated at Grimes Graves.*

TOP FOUR NEW STONE AGE
FLINT MINES

1 **Spiennes**, Mons, Belgium, 4300–2200 BCE
Area: 100 hectares; **Shafts:** 5000 just in the central zone, called Petit Spiennes (14 hectares)

2 **Krzemionki**, Poland, 3900–1600 BCE
Area: 78.5 hectares; **Shafts:** 4000

3 **Grimes Graves**, Norfolk, Britain, 3000–1150 BCE
Area: 37 hectares; **Shafts:** at least 433

4 **Cissbury**, West Sussex, Britain, 3000–2100 BCE
Area: 26 hectares; **Shafts:** 200

⓳ ▶ Crafts

Traders and settlers from Europe brought pottery making to the British Isles during the New Stone Age, and the skill quickly spread. The first pots and bowls were simply decorated. Meanwhile stone carving was becoming more complex.

POTTERY MANUFACTURE

Making pottery requires two things – clay and fire. Firing clay (heating it to high temperatures) makes it hard and can make it waterproof. This can be done on an open fire, but usually happens inside an oven called a kiln. Experts have found a few circular structures from New Stone Age times that might have been kilns.

▲ A reconstruction of a New Stone Age kiln made from turf. The top has been taken off to reveal the fire inside.

◀ This carved chalk object, found in North Yorkshire, was made about 2600 to 2000 bce. It is decorated with abstract patterns and faces.

ORNAMENTAL OBJECTS

Beautiful stone objects have been found in New Stone Age tombs and other places. It is not always obvious what they were for – perhaps they were used in special rituals or maybe they were just lovely to look at!

▶ This carved stone object was found at Skara Brae (see pages 28–29). No one knows how it was used.

Ötzi the Iceman

In 1991, two hikers discovered a frozen body high in the Alps on the border between Austria and Italy. Little did they realize that this ice mummy was about 5300 years old! The body belonged to a man from the Copper Age (see page 40), now known as Ötzi the Iceman.

▲ This photo shows Ötzi's body during its removal from the ice in September 1991.

◄ Experts think Ötzi may have looked like this. His clothes were made of leather, skins and grass.

ÖTZI'S BODY

Ice had preserved Ötzi's body very well. Experts found that he had died at the age of 40. He had a fractured skull and a recent arrow wound in his shoulder. His digestive system contained traces of wheat bran, fruits, roots and meat from deer and chamois (a goat-antelope).

▼ Ötzi was found on this mountain in the Ötztal Alps between Austria and Italy.

METAL CLUES

When Ötzi was alive, people in Europe were beginning to work metal. These skills did not arrive in Britain until later. Ötzi's hair contained traces of copper and arsenic, so he may have worked copper. His belongings included a copper axe.

◄ Replica of Ötzi's axe with its copper blade.

35

Tombs

New Stone Age people took a lot of care over burying their dead. Now that they were living in settled communities, they marked burial places with stone monuments for all to see. Many different kinds of New Stone Age tombs still stand today.

South Korea has about 16,000 New Stone Age dolmens (tombs).

PASSAGE GRAVES

Many New Stone Age tombs have a passageway that leads to the burial chamber (or chambers). Tombs such as these are called **passage graves**. The whole tomb would have been covered with earth or stone. Today, the coverings have often weathered away.

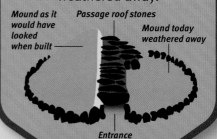

Mound as it would have looked when built

Passage roof stones

Mound today weathered away

Entrance

◄ Five huge stone slabs form a gateway to this portal tomb or dolmen at Poulnabrone in County Clare, Ireland.

PORTAL TOMBS

Some tombs have dramatic stone entrances, or portals. These tombs are known as portal tombs or **dolmens**. The top slab is called a capstone. Not all dolmens were tombs. Some might have been put up as markers to show the boundary of a family's land.

Earthworks

New Stone Age earthworks take the form of mounds, **barrows** and henges (see below). Some were built as tombs, others were places of worship and some remain a mystery!

▼ *Standing 37 metres tall, Silbury Hill is the largest human-made mound in Europe. It does not contain a tomb.*

TYPES OF HENGES

Some henges contain stone or timber circles. Stonehenge (see pages 38–39) has stone circles. Just 3.2 kilometres away, Woodhenge had six rings of timber posts. In north Yorkshire, Thornborough simply has a line of three huge, circular earthworks (one of them overgrown with trees).

◀ *Each of the three Thornborough henges is about 240 metres across.*

WHAT'S IN A NAME?

Earthwork
Any large bank of soil made by humans, including mounds, barrows and henges.

Mound
An earthwork where the earth creates a hill. Mounds were built to cover tombs or for defence.

Barrow
Like mounds, barrows were earthworks built to cover tombs. New Stone Age barrows were often oval-shaped, and known as long barrows.

Henge
A circular earthwork with an outer bank and inner ditch.

Newgrange

Newgrange's entrance stone weighs about the same as an African elephant!

The circular mound at Newgrange in County Meath, Ireland, is one of the largest in the British Isles. Built about 3200 BCE, it was designed so that at dawn on the winter **solstice** (the shortest day of the year) sunlight would shine through an opening above the entrance, filling the main chamber with light.

ASTRONOMICAL KNOW-HOW

Many New Stone Age monuments were designed to create a special effect at a certain time of year. The central chamber at Maes Howe on Orkney also lights up at the winter solstice. New Stone Age people must have had some understanding of how the Sun's position in relation to the Earth changed over the year.

▲ Above the entrance stone is the opening where sunlight enters on the winter solstice.

▼ Newgrange's dazzling white quartz wall was built between 1967 and 1974, when the site was being reconstructed.

INSIDE NEWGRANGE

The Newgrange passage grave (see page 34) measures 76 metres across, and is made of clay and grass. A stone wall surrounds it. Inside is a passageway, a mound and three smaller chambers.

▲ A stone passageway leads from the entrance to the central chamber.

Standing stones and menhirs

With no machinery to help them, people in the New Stone Age put up extraordinary stone monuments. Some were just one lone stone, known as a menhir; other standing stones were arranged in groups. Sometimes the stones have patterns on them.

◄ *Some standing stones, such as this one at Avebury, are so big that in medieval times people thought they were the work of giants!*

◄ *Avebury in Wiltshire, England, has three stone circles. The outer one is Europe's largest stone circle – it is more than 330 metres across.*

FRENCH SITES

France has more than 1600 standing stone sites, and half of them are in Brittany. The largest French menhir, called *Grand Menhir Brisé* (Great Broken Menhir) stood more than 20 metres tall and weighed more than 280 tonnes, but it now lies in pieces.

▲ *Carnac in Brittany, France, has more than 3000 standing stones. Most are carefully grouped in rows or circles.*

SACRED STONES

No one can be certain why people put up standing stones. Some mark a spot where human remains or ashes were buried, sometimes with precious objects (grave goods). Stone circles were probably places for religious ceremonies

Stonehenge

Stonehenge on Salisbury Plain, Wiltshire, is Britain's most famous New Stone Age site. The first monument there was a henge earthwork – a low, circular bank of earth with a ditch. People buried the ashes of their dead around this earthwork. After about 500 years, the circles of huge stones were put up.

▼ Stonehenge as it looks today.

A SNUG FIT

Workers bashed and smoothed the stones using hammerstones. They gave the tops of the upright stones bumps called tenons. These tenons fitted into the mortice holes they chipped out of the lintel (horizontal) stones. The lintels had tongue-and-groove joints so they fitted snugly together.

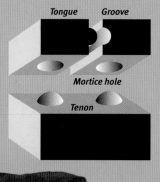

Tongue   Groove

Mortice hole

Tenon

▼ Stonehenge would have been visible to people for miles around. Perhaps it was a temple for worshippers or a burial ground.

KEY EVENTS

c. 3000 BCE
Earthwork built at Stonehenge.

c. 2600 BCE
Bluestones put into position.

RAISING THE STONES

The smaller stones, called bluestones because they look bluish when they are wet, came from the Preseli Hills in Wales, more than 250 kilometres away. The larger sarsen stones were from the Marlborough Downs, 32 kilometres away. No one knows for sure how they were transported. They were probably floated down rivers on massive rafts and hauled over land on logs.

Moving the stones.

Raising the stones.

Fixing in position.

Bluestone horseshoe (small stones)
Sunrise on summer solstice
Bluestone circle
Avenue
Heel stone
Altar stone
Bank
Ditch
Sunset on winter solstice
Sarsen circle
Sarsen horseshoe

▲ When it was finished, Stonehenge had two outer circles of stones and two inner half-circles, or horseshoes.

A GIANT CALENDAR

Stonehenge's stones are positioned to mark two important days. At sunrise on the summer solstice (the longest day of the year), the sun rises between the heel stone and the place where there was a matching stone. At sunset on the winter solstice (the shortest day of the year), it sinks between the gap in the central horseshoe.

c. 2500 BCE
Sarsens in position and bluestones arranged.

c. 2300 BCE
Bluestones re-arranged and avenue built.

THE BRONZE AGE

The end of the Stone Age came when people learned to make things out of metal. In Britain, this happened about 2500 BCE. The Copper Age (Chalcolithic) began when they found out how to shape copper. Next they worked tin and gold. By 2200 BCE, they had discovered that mixing copper and tin made a harder, more useful metal called bronze. The Bronze Age had begun. It ended in about 800 BCE, when people learned how to make an even stronger metal – iron.

▲ One way miners got copper from stone was by smashing it out. They used heavy hammer stones, sometimes fixed to leather straps.

FIRST BRONZE

Bronze was first made about 3200 BCE in what is now Turkey.

▲ The Isleham Hoard contains spearheads, swords and other weapons. Different clans fought during the Bronze Age, so weapons were very important.

HUGE HOARD

The biggest collection of Bronze Age bronze ever found in Britain dates to about 1075 BCE. The Isleham Hoard from Cambridgeshire, eastern England, contains more than 6500 pieces of bronze. As well as swords, arrows, axes and knives, there are pieces of sheet metal that had not yet been 'worked' (made into something).

KEY EVENTS

c. 2500 BCE
People in Britain learn how to work metal (see pages 42–43). The Copper Age begins.

Beaker culture (see page 44) arrives in Britain.

c. 2300 BCE
The Amesbury Archer is alive (see page 45).

c. 2200 BCE
People in Britain are working bronze. The Bronze Age begins.

CHIEFS AND CHANGE

Society in Britain changed during the Bronze Age. The first rulers or chieftains gained power by controlling precious resources, such as mines or farmland. They grew rich through trade with other clan leaders.

▼ Traders from Europe imported some metal, but Britain also mined its own supplies.

▲ Chieftans showed off their status with fine possessions. This gold cup (c. 1700 bce) was found at Rillaton in Cornwall, England.

SCOTLAND

NORTH SEA

IRELAND

Great Orme

North Ferriby

Mold

Holme I Seahenge

Isleham

WALES

ENGLAND

Amesbury

Dover

MAP KEY

→ Tin

→ Amber

→ Copper

→ Gold and crafted goods

Bronze was found all over Britain and Ireland.

▲ This shield (c. 1300–1000 bce) was beaten from a single disk of bronze. It is about 50 centimetres across and just seven millimetres thick.

2049 bce	**c. 2030 bce**	**c. 1800 bce**	**c. 1550 bce**	**c. 1075 bce**
Holme I ('Seahenge') is constructed (see page 53).	Ferriby Boat 3 is in use (see page 51).	Copper mining begins at Great Orme in Wales (see pages 42–43).	The Dover boat and the Must Farm boats are made (see pages 50–51).	The bronze treasures of the Isleham Hoard date to this time (see pages 76–77).

Mining and metalworking

Metals such as gold, copper and tin are found as minerals in rocks, either deep underground or on the surface. Gold is also found in streams. Ireland was rich in gold and copper, Wales had copper and gold, and Cornwall had copper and tin.

▲ Copper is found in minerals such as malachite and azurite. Malachite is a beautiful bright green; azurite is blue.

EXTRACTING ORE

Bronze Age miners lit fires either underground or next to a rock face to heat the rock. Then they threw on water to crack the rock so they could take away chunks of ore (rock that contains metal). In areas of softer rock, they gouged out the minerals with pointed bits of bone.

▶ If miners could not smash out the copper ore, they used fire to heat the rock until it cracked.

Copper ore extracted from rocks

GREAT ORME

One of Europe's largest Bronze Age copper mines was at Great Orme in north Wales. It was a huge complex of horizontal and vertical tunnels, dug to a depth of 70 metres.

Some copper mine tunnels were so small they must have been mined by children.

WORKING WITH METAL

To extract copper, people first smashed the ore with stones. Then they heated the crushed ore. At 1083°C, the copper melted and collected in a bowl at the bottom of the furnace. When the copper cooled, it could be hammered into shapes. Bronze was worked the same way, but by mixing tin and copper ores or metals.

METAL OBJECTS

The earliest artefacts made of copper and tin were axes, daggers and awls. Stone tools continued to be used as well. Only powerful people had objects made of bronze or gold. Having rare and precious belongings showed how important they were.

▶An Early Bronze Age axehead.

▲ A Bronze Age awl – a pointed tool used for marking surfaces or making holes in wood.

Metalworker pours molten metal into a mould

Crushed ore being heated in furnace

Bellows

Wood for the fire

CAPE OF GOLD

In 1833, some **quarry** workers at Mold in north Wales found a Bronze Age burial mound. Inside were the remains of a spectacular cape of thin, gold foil. It was in hundreds of pieces when it was found, but has since been painstakingly put back together.

▲ The Mold cape was made between 1900 and 1600 bce. It was found with other precious objects, including amber beads.

Beaker culture

Metalworking appeared in Britain at about the same time as a new style of pottery. Bell-shaped beakers were the work of people belonging to the Beaker culture. Experts think that they brought their metalworking knowledge to Britain from mainland Europe, as well as their pots.

WHO WERE THE BEAKER PEOPLE?

The Beaker people appeared in western Europe about 2800 BCE. They are named after their distinctive pots, which were shaped like bells and were decorated with lines. Some of the pots were used as beakers to hold drinks. Others were used as burial urns and held people's ashes.

▼ A reconstructed Bronze Age beaker from Avebury, England.

▶ This is the West Kennet Long Barrow, near Avebury, England, where a complete, unbroken bell beaker was found. It was made soon after 2500 bce.

▲ This map shows the areas where Beaker culture flourished in the Early Bronze Age.

SPREADING CULTURE

Experts cannot agree exactly where Beaker culture began, but it spread across Europe. This happened because people were starting to have more contact with each other. When they met neighbouring peoples, they shared ideas. In this way, Beaker-style pottery and metalworking eventually reached Britain.

The Amesbury Archer

The Amesbury Archer is a 40-year-old man whose remains were found in a grave near Stonehenge. He died in the Copper Age, about 2300 BCE. He was buried with a rich collection of objects, including five Beaker pots.

▲ The Archer's copper knives were from mainland Europe. He must have travelled or had trading contacts there.

GRAVE GOODS

The Amesbury Archer must have been an important man. He was buried with the largest collection of equipment ever found in a Beaker grave. He also had gold hair ornaments.

◄ The Amesbury Archer died in Wiltshire, but that is not where he was born. Scientists who have examined him think he may have come from the Swiss Alps.

▲ The Archer's Companion was 20 to 25 years old. His grave contained a pair of gold hair ornaments just like the Archer's.

THE ARCHER'S COMPANION

The Archer's grave was discovered in 2002 by workers building a new school. A nearby grave contained the remains of a younger man, known as the Archer's Companion. Both men had unusual feet bones, so they were probably related.

There were 100 objects in the grave of the Amesbury Archer.

Bronze Age barrows

Instead of building large, communal burial mounds, as people had in the New Stone Age, Bronze Age mourners buried important people individually under small, round mounds called barrows. This shows how society was changing, with certain individuals becoming more important and powerful than others.

SIGNS OF THE PAST

Over the years, farmers have levelled (made flat) many Bronze Age barrows. Even so, it is still possible to see their outlines when viewing the land from the air.

▲ Many of the barrows at Winterbourne Abbas in Dorset have been flattened or damaged by ploughing.

▼ Round barrows on Overton Hill, Wiltshire.

BARROW CEMETERIES

Normanton Down in Wiltshire is a barrow cemetery that includes a New Stone Age long barrow as well as more than forty Bronze Age round barrows. One is the Bush Barrow, excavated in 1808. It contained a man's body, along with a bronze and copper dagger, a gold belt hook, a bronze axe and a stone mace (ceremonial staff).

▲ Normanton Down barrows in Wiltshire, England, in snow.

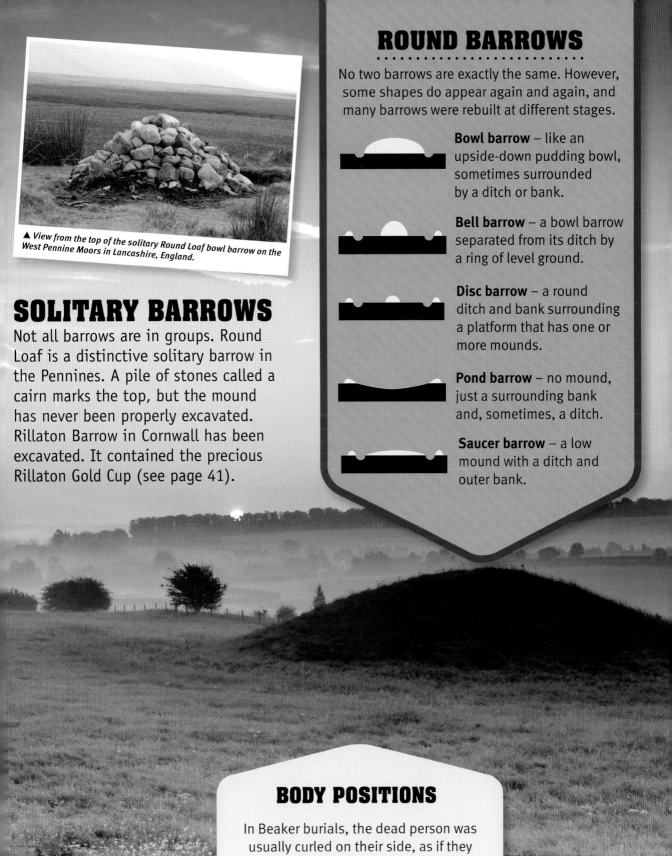

ROUND BARROWS

No two barrows are exactly the same. However, some shapes do appear again and again, and many barrows were rebuilt at different stages.

Bowl barrow – like an upside-down pudding bowl, sometimes surrounded by a ditch or bank.

Bell barrow – a bowl barrow separated from its ditch by a ring of level ground.

Disc barrow – a round ditch and bank surrounding a platform that has one or more mounds.

Pond barrow – no mound, just a surrounding bank and, sometimes, a ditch.

Saucer barrow – a low mound with a ditch and outer bank.

▲ View from the top of the solitary Round Loaf bowl barrow on the West Pennine Moors in Lancashire, England.

SOLITARY BARROWS

Not all barrows are in groups. Round Loaf is a distinctive solitary barrow in the Pennines. A pile of stones called a cairn marks the top, but the mound has never been properly excavated. Rillaton Barrow in Cornwall has been excavated. It contained the precious Rillaton Gold Cup (see page 41).

BODY POSITIONS

In Beaker burials, the dead person was usually curled on their side, as if they were asleep. In round barrow burials, the dead person is on their back or there is an urn containing their ashes.

Everyday life

Bronze Age people lived in settlements of circular roundhouses. Each house had a timber framework, walls made of **wattle and daub**, and a thatched roof. This basic house design lasted through the Iron Age until the coming of the Romans.

FARMING

People began to organize the land into fields for growing crops or grazing animals. They marked the boundaries of their field systems with stones or boulders.

▼ *This modern reconstruction of a Bronze Age roundhouse is at Flag Fen, Cambridgeshire, England (see page 52).*

▼ *Each roundhouse was home to probably one family. Even the biggest settlements had no more than about 20 houses.*

INSIDE A ROUNDHOUSE

The hearth was at the centre of the roundhouse. The fire was kept alight all day and all night. It provided warmth and light, and was used for cooking. The smoke escaped through the thatched roof.

CLOTHING

Bronze Age people knew how to weave wool into cloth. Men probably wore a tunic with leggings or a kilt, and a cloak. Women probably wore short tunics and woollen skirts.

HISTORY OF THE HORSE

Horses had been domesticated in the grasslands of Eurasia about 4000 to 3500 BCE. Chariot burials found in the Ural Mountains date to about 2000 BCE – they contain the remains of horses attached to chariots. Horses quickly spread west across Europe.

Rise of the horse

During the Late Bronze Age, horses became an important means of transport. They pulled wheeled vehicles, and could also be ridden by warriors.

▲ Farmers first grazed ponies on Dartmoor, southwest England, during the Bronze Age, about 1500 bce, and they still graze them there today.

▲ Bronze Age artists celebrated the horse by carving its image into hillsides. This chalk horse is at Uffington in Oxfordshire.

IN PEACE AND WAR

Horses were useful to farmers because they could pull ploughs and carts, but their speed made them especially valuable in times of war, when they were used to pull chariots. There was a lot of unrest towards the end of the Bronze Age, as neighbouring chiefs clashed over territory and resources.

▲ This bronze statue from the 1300s bce is one of the earliest models of a horse-drawn chariot in Europe. It was found in Denmark.

Bronze Age boats

In 2011, archaeologists found the remains of eight Bronze Age boats at Must Farm in Cambridgeshire. These have been dated to about 1500 BCE. Britain has other examples of Bronze Age boats, too.

Britain's oldest log boat was found in Ireland — it dates back to about 1940 BCE.

BOAT FINDS

This map shows some of the places where Bronze Age boats have been found.

Addergoole bog Galway, site of oldest log boat

North Ferriby boats

Must Farm boats

IRELAND

BRITAIN

Dover boat

Salcombe trading ship

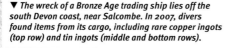

▼ The wreck of a Bronze Age trading ship lies off the south Devon coast, near Salcombe. In 2007, divers found items from its cargo, including rare copper ingots (top row) and tin ingots (middle and bottom rows).

▲ These rare pieces of Bronze Age gold jewellery were also found on the Salcombe shipwreck.

THE MUST FARM BOATS

The eight boats at Must Farm are dugout log boats, made from oak, lime and field maple. The largest is almost 9 metres long. The boats were used for fishing and moving cargo around the fens. It looks as if they were deliberately sunk, but no one is sure why.

CROSS-CHANNEL FERRY

The Dover boat, which dates to 1550 BCE, was built from oak planks sewn together with thin, bendy yew branches. It probably ferried tin, bronze and other goods across the English Channel. No one can be sure of the boat's exact size. Experts dug up about 9.5 metres of it, but had to leave the rest in case they damaged local homes.

▲ One of the Must Farm Bronze Age log boats. After it was found, it was sprayed with wax to stop it rotting.

CONTACT WITH EUROPE

New Stone Age people used boats to bring farm animals to Britain from mainland Europe. By the Copper Age, Britain had trade links with the continent. Objects found in Beaker graves had come from overseas.

▼ The English Channel at Dover, where the Dover boat would have come and gone loaded with cargo.

THE FERRIBY BOATS

Three Bronze Age boats were found at Ferriby, on the Humber estuary in Yorkshire, England. They are older than the Dover boat, but also built from oak planks. The oldest boat, Ferriby 3, dates back to 2030 BCE.

▲ In 2013, Britain's first-ever full size replica of a sea-going Bronze Age boat made its maiden voyage. It was based on one of the Ferriby boats.

Bronze Age religion

Grave goods show us that Bronze Age people may have believed in an afterlife – they thought they would need belongings after their death. At some Bronze Age sites, archaeologists have also found objects that may have been offerings to the gods.

No one can really be sure what happened when people threw offerings into waterways. Perhaps they were alone and chanted private prayers. Perhaps they were taking part in ceremonies led by priests.

▼ *Reconstruction of the causeway (walkway) at Flag Fen.*

▲ *Offerings at Flag Fen included jewellery (above), swords, daggers and fragments of pottery.*

FLAG FEN

Flag Fen is a Late Bronze Age site near Peterborough, England. It is close to where the Must Farm boats were found (see page 50). During the Bronze Age, a one-kilometre-long wooden causeway (walkway) crossed the marsh at Flag Fen. People threw precious objects into the marsh from the causeway. These were probably gifts for the gods.

▼ *The causeway was made of thousands of large wooden posts arranged in five rows. The pencil-like tips of the posts were driven through the mud into the firmer ground below. Between the posts, timbers were built up horizontally. These provided the surface for walking along.*

The Flag Fen causeway was used as a ritual site for more than 1200 years.

Settlement | Island | Wetland fen | Causeway

Sacred circles

Many of the stone circles and other sacred sites from the New Stone Age were still in use during the Bronze Age. People also continued to put up new stone and timber circles.

'SEAHENGE'

Holme I is a timber circle that was discovered on the beach at Holme-next-the-Sea in Norfolk. Nicknamed 'Seahenge', it consists of 55 oak posts arranged in an oval around an upturned oak stump. The trees were all cut down in 2049 BCE. Experts think that the central stump might have been used for 'sky burials' – a practice where dead bodies are placed on a platform until they decompose.

▼ Holme I, before it was excavated and transported to the visitor centre at Flag Fen, where it is preserved in freshwater.

▼ Holme II has not been excavated. It has been left where it is in the sea.

ALL AT SEA

Holme II was found 100 metres to the east of Holme I. It dates from 2400 to 2300 BCE. The site has two circles, one inside the other, surrounding two large, central oak logs.

THE IRON AGE

In Britain, the first iron objects were produced about 1000 BCE. By 800 BCE, iron was the main metal being made. The Iron Age in Britain lasted from 800 BCE until the arrival of the Romans in the first century CE. During this time, **Celtic** art and culture from mainland Europe reached Britain.

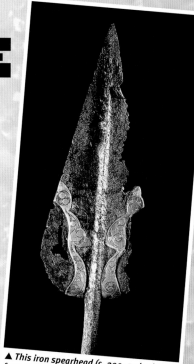

▲ This iron spearhead (c. 200–50 bce) was found in the River Thames. It is decorated with shiny strips of bronze.

▼ The people who lived at Hallstatt were buried with fine objects. This bronze container came from one of the richest graves.

EARLY CENTRES

Some of Europe's first-known Iron Age settlements were around Hallstatt in the Austrian Alps and date to before 800 BCE. The people lived in **hill forts**, mined salt and worked bronze and iron. They also traded with other peoples, including the Ancient Greeks, the Phoenicians (from the eastern Mediterranean coast) and the Etruscans (from western Italy). Their graves contain luxurious items of gold, bronze, amber, ivory and silk.

KEY EVENTS

c. 800 to 500 BCE
The Hallstatt culture flourishes in central Europe (see above).

800 BCE to c. 50 CE
The hill fort called Maiden Castle is built in Dorset, England (see page 59).

500 to 100 BCE
The La Tène culture flourishes in central Europe (see page 64).

c. 350 BCE
Celtic art arrives in Britain (see pages 64–65).

GOING UP!

By the first century BCE, the population of Britain probably topped one million.

COINS

The first coins were produced in Britain in the 100s BCE. Some were stamped with the names of rulers or the name of the place where they were made.

▲ Iron Age gold coin

SCOTLAND

IRELAND

BRITAIN

GAUL

MAP KEY

Hallstatt core

Hallstatt influence

La Tène core

Boundary of La Tène influence

● La Tène, SWITZERLAND

● Hallstatt, AUSTRIA

▲ This La Tène style head was discovered at a site near Prague in the Czech Republic.

▲ Celtic culture spread out from Hallstatt (800–500 bce) and, later, from La Tène (500–100 bce), a site beside Lake Neuchâtel in Switzerland.

▲ This is a modern view of Hallstatt Lake, Austria. Celtic culture and art first flourished around its shores.

c. 300 BCE
The Wetwang chariot burial takes place in east Yorkshire (see page 70).

The bog person Clonycavan Man is alive (see page 71).

c. 80 to 60 BCE
Production of gold coins starts in Britain.

55 and 54 BCE
Julius Caesar makes two failed attempts to invade Britain (see page 56).

43 BCE
The Romans successfully invade Britain and the Iron Age ends (see pages 74–75).

The Celtic culture of the period is called La Tène, after a site in Switzerland.

During the Iron Age, Celtic-speaking peoples spread out across Europe. They were made up of many tribes or family groups (see page 57), but the Romans gave them one single name – the **Gauls**. This was because they lived in the region that the Romans called Gallia or Gaul (modern France, Luxembourg and Belgium).

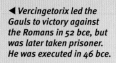

◀ Vercingetorix led the Gauls to victory against the Romans in 52 bce, but was later taken prisoner. He was executed in 46 bce.

▶ In 387 bce, Brennus captured all of the city of Rome except for the Capitoline Hill. It was protected by geese that honked the alarm!

GAULS V. ROMANS

Over the years, there were many clashes between the Romans and the Gauls.

390 BCE
Gallic chieftain Brennus defeats the Romans at the Battle of the Allia.

225 BCE
Romans defeat the Gauls of northern Italy at Telamon.

101 BCE
Roman general Marius defeats invading Gauls at Vercellae.

58 to 51 BCE
Julius Caesar conquers Gaul, just before his attempt to conquer Britain.

Brennus

FAMOUS GAULS

Brennus (4th century BCE)
Chief of the Senones tribe, he sacked the city of Rome.

Vercingetorix (c. 82 to 46 BCE)
Chief of the Arverni tribe, he led a united revolt against Julius Caesar.

Commius (1st century BCE)
Chief of the Atrebates tribe, he moved from Gaul to Britain.

Tribal kingdoms

In Britain, the end of the Bronze Age was not a peaceful time. Different clans or groups often clashed violently, all wanting to control precious resources. This continued into the Iron Age. Although many people in Britain were speaking the same Celtic languages as each other, some were fierce rivals.

▲ The Roman historian Tacitus (56–117 ce) wrote about the tribes living in Britain at the time of the Roman conquest.

TRIBAL STRUCTURE

A tribe is a group of people who have family connections with each other. Over time, smaller family groups became connected to each other through marriages, and became part of larger tribes. The Brigantes, for example, was a large tribe in northern England. Each tribe was led by its own chieftain, king or queen.

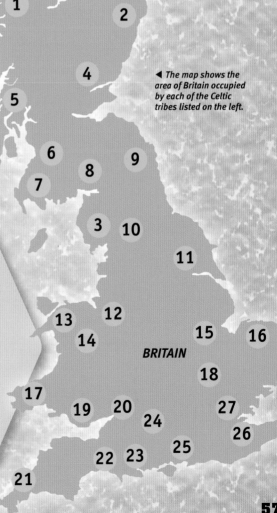

◄ The map shows the area of Britain occupied by each of the Celtic tribes listed on the left.

BRITAIN

TRIBAL NAMES

The names that we use for Celtic tribes, listed below, are not actually Celtic, but Latin – the language of the Romans. That's because the Celtic peoples did not have writing, while the Romans did.

1 Caledones
2 Taexali
3 Carvetii
4 Venicones
5 Epidii
6 Damnonii
7 Novantae
8 Selgovae
9 Votadini
10 Brigantes
11 Parisi
12 Cornovii
13 Deceangli
14 Ordovices
15 Corieltauvi
16 Iceni
17 Demetae
18 Catuvellauni
19 Silures
20 Dubunni
21 Dumnonii
22 Durotriges
23 Belgae
24 Atrebates
25 Regni
26 Cantiaci
27 Trinovantes

Hill forts

CAMELOT

The 16th-century historian John Leland believed that Cadbury Castle, a hill fort in Somerset, was the site of legendary King Arthur's castle, Camelot.

▲ Cadbury Castle near Yeovil, Somerset, has four terraced earthwork banks and ditches.

Hill forts were settlements that were built on top of hills. They first appeared in the Late Bronze Age. During the Iron Age, more than 3000 hill forts were built across Britain. Being on a hilltop was a good natural defence because it meant enemies could be seen approaching from a long way off. Later, further defences were added, such as earthworks and walls that followed the contours (curves) of the hillside.

▲ The warriors who attacked hill forts were armed with spears and axes. They carried shields like this one.

A SAFE PLACE

Hill forts provided a refuge in times of war. People abandoned their fields and herded their animals up to the safety of the fort. From there, approaching enemies could be picked off with spears and slingshots. Some areas of Britain had many hill forts in sight of one another. Inhabitants could send warnings to each other, using light beacons or smoke signals.

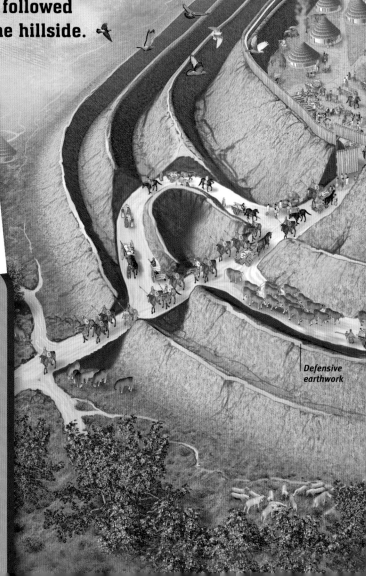

Defensive earthwork

BIG AND SMALL

Some hill forts were used only in time of war, but some were settlements. They contained roundhouses, stockades (fenced areas) for livestock, and granaries for storing grain. Bigger ones also had markets, iron workshops and places of worship.

▼ *This illustration shows what a large Iron Age hill fort would have been like.*

▲ *Danebury is probably Britain's most thoroughly excavated hill fort. Finds there tell archaeologists a lot about how hill forts were used. Danebury was in use for about 500 years.*

▼ *Rings of banks and ditches protected the Iron Age inhabitants of Maiden Castle.*

MAIDEN CASTLE

Britain's largest hill fort is Maiden Castle in Dorset. The site had been used for farming in the New Stone Age and Bronze Age. About 700 BCE, a simple hill fort was built, covering about 6.4 hectares. In 450 BCE, the fort was greatly expanded to enclose 19 hectares, making it one of the largest hill forts in Europe.

40 Iron Age farms

During the Iron Age, most people lived by farming. New, strong iron tools made lighter work of breaking up the soil and harvesting crops, so people were able to produce more food than in earlier times.

▼ *This is what an Iron Age farm may have looked like.*

Farmers had iron axes for clearing the land. The trees they chopped down were used to build homes or make tool handles. Iron shovels and ploughs were used to work the soil. In the farmhouse, grinding grain into flour became easier with the arrival of the rotary quern, about 400 BCE.

Grain

Top stone, turned by handle

Grinding stone

Handle

▲ *Rotary quern*

CROPS AND LIVESTOCK

The main crops were still wheat and barley, which were slowly becoming hardier (stronger and better at surviving cold weather) and producing fatter grains. People also grew peas, beans, cabbages and parsnips, as well as flax for the fibres in its stems. These were spun to make linen (a type of cloth). People kept cattle, sheep and pigs for meat, manure, milk, leather and wool.

▲ *Iron Age piglets would have looked like these – stripy rather than pink.*

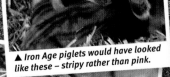

▲ *By the Iron Age, emmer wheat (shown here) was being sown as well as spelt. Both were very tough but didn't produce much grain.*

Ironworking

Iron ore was plentiful in most parts of Britain. This meant that iron was cheap, even though the metal itself was harder to extract than copper or tin. By the end of the Iron Age, iron was being used for all sorts of things, from tiny rivets to impressive swords.

SMELTING IRON

The process of smelting iron was similar to how copper and tin were smelted, but required much higher temperatures. The crushed iron ore was heated with charcoal inside clay furnaces called bloomeries. The iron, or 'bloom', melted down to the bottom of the furnace. Smelters shaped this iron into ingots (oblong blocks).

▼ This 19th-century etching imagines what an Iron Age forge would have looked like.

THE WORK OF A BLACKSMITH

The forge was a hot, smoky and dangerous place to work. The blacksmith shaped ingots of raw iron or old scrap metal. First he heated the iron over a charcoal fire until it was red-hot and beginning to soften. Then, using hammer and tongs, he battered it into shape. Joining pieces of iron required higher temperatures – the iron had to be heated until it was white-hot.

▲ This is one of a pair of iron fire dogs. It propped up logs in the fireplace, so air could flow under them and the fire would burn properly.

An Iron Age village

During the Iron Age, people carried on living in roundhouses as they had during the Bronze Age. No one really knows why Britons had a tradition of circular homes. Elsewhere in Europe, people were living in rectangular houses.

▶ *Most cooking was done in a cauldron, which hung from a tripod over the fire.*

HUGE HOUSE

Most roundhouses were about six metres across. However, an Iron Age roundhouse found in Dorset was 15 metres across, giving it more floor space than most modern homes!

HOME, SWEET HOME

The roundhouse usually contained just one room, though some larger houses had an upper floor in the loft space. The hearth was still at the centre of the home, and there might be a simple clay oven as well as a fireplace. There were no windows – all the light came from the fire, oil lamps or the door when it was open during the day.

▲ *This wool has been coloured with natural plant dyes used in the Iron Age: woad (blue), madder (red) and weld (yellow).*

VILLAGE COMMUNITIES

Jobs were divided up between the community. Making charcoal was an important task. Blacksmiths made tools, weapons and everyday objects. Some people made dyes from plants, other people tanned leather, and there were specialist potters, too (see page 65).

In some roundhouses the door faced east, so the morning sun could shine in.

Crannogs, brochs and wheelhouses

Not all Iron Age homes in Britain were the same. People living in Scotland and Ireland had their own designs for houses. Some of these developed because people needed to defend their living space.

WATERY DEFENCES

Crannogs were roundhouses that stood on jetties or human-made islands. Being built over water made them easy to defend. Some were made of timber, and others were made of stone.

▼ *This modern reconstruction of a crannog stands on Loch Tay, Scotland. During the Iron Age, the loch had 18 crannogs.*

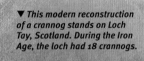

▲ *Large wheelhouses, such as this one on the Shetland Islands, housed several families.*

BROCHS

Brochs were another kind of building that could be defended from attack. Built across northern Scotland, they were circular towers with thick, dry-stone walls. Some of the larger brochs had inner and outer walls, with a winding stone stairway between them leading to the upper floors.

WHEELHOUSES

Wheelhouses were unique to Scotland. These stone buildings were round and had a central hearth. Walls, arranged like the spokes of a wheel, divided the building into small separate rooms.

Celtic art and craft

Iron Age artists and craftworkers produced beautiful metalwork, pottery and jewellery. They often decorated their pieces with distinctive, swirling designs made up of circles and spirals.

LA TÈNE DESIGNS

The La Tène culture flourished from 500 to 100 BCE. Celtic art from this time began to use particular patterns or motifs: spirals and scrolls, as well as leafy tendrils, vines and flowers.

Triskele   *Spiral*

▼ This Celtic horned helmet (c. 150–50 bce) has plant-like decorations in the La Tène style.

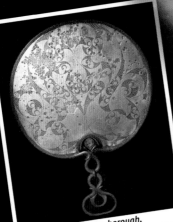

▲ This mirror from Desborough, Northamptonshire, dates to 50 bce–50 ce. Its other side would have been polished to a high shine to give a reflection.

OBJECTS OF BEAUTY

Metalworkers used bronze for decorative objects and iron for day-to-day artefacts. Some of the finest bronze creations are bowls and hand mirrors – these were intricately engraved and would have been highly prized.

BURIED TREASURE

Jewellery worn by Iron Age men and women has been discovered in treasure hoards (hidden stores of treasure, see pages 76–77). Some hoards may have been left as offerings to the gods. Perhaps others were hidden in times of danger and not found again. Archaeologists have found silver and gold bracelets, brooches and torcs (thick, metal neck rings).

▲ This magnificent torc (c. 75 bce) from Snettisham, Norfolk, is made up of 64 fine, interwoven threads of gold mixed with silver.

CELTIC POTTERY

For most of the Iron Age, pots were made by hand-shaping the clay, or coiling it round. Then, towards the end of the Iron Age, the potter's wheel arrived. This gave potters more control, and pots became more symmetrical.

▲ These Iron Age terracotta pots include two bowls, a cooking pot and two jugs.

OTHER CRAFTS

At home, people wove wool and linen into cloth on a loom. In their workshops, tanners made leather from animal skins. First they treated the skins with salt and special chemicals, then they soaked them and dried them out. The process preserved the skin so it would not rot, and left it flexible enough to be stitched and made into shoes, belts or shields.

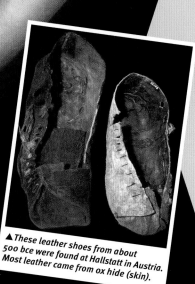

▲ These leather shoes from about 500 bce were found at Hallstatt in Austria. Most leather came from ox hide (skin).

Beliefs and religion

As in the Bronze Age, Iron Age people believed in spirits that were connected to the natural world. People threw offerings into lakes, rivers and bogs, hoping that the spirits would protect them. They also had priests called **druids**.

▼ *Druids were spiritual leaders, and also teachers, healers and judges. In this ceremony, a druid throws a shield into the river as an offering.*

GODS AND GODDESSES

Across Celtic Europe, hundreds of different gods and goddesses were worshipped. Some were local to a particular place, but others were worshipped everywhere. Many gods were linked by festivals to the farming year, which affected everyone. In May, a great fire festival called Beltane was held to honour the god Belenus. Fires were lit in the belief that the god would then protect their cattle, before they were let out into the fields for the summer.

CELTIC GODS AND GODDESSES

Artio goddess of bears.
Belenus god of keeping cattle, also linked to the Sun and fires.
Brigit goddess of healing, poetry, fertility and cattle.
Cernunnos god of fertility, harvests and the Underworld.
Coventina goddess of springs and wells.
Epona goddess of horses.
Fagus god of beech trees.
Lugus god of the arts.
Morrigan goddess of war, who took the form of a crow.
Robor god of oak trees.

Druids often held their ceremonies in sacred groves of trees.

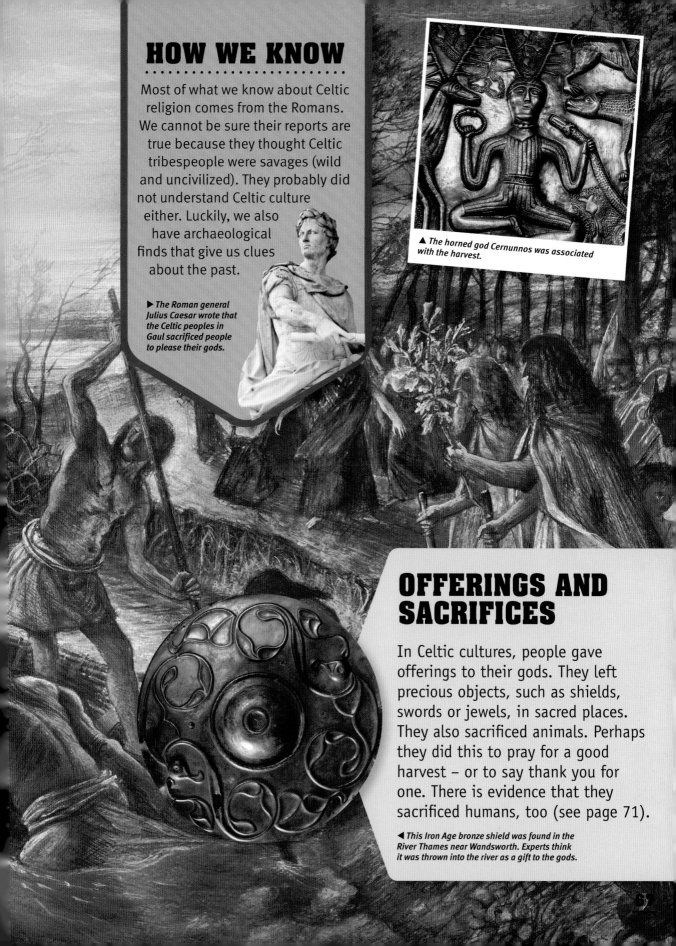

HOW WE KNOW

Most of what we know about Celtic religion comes from the Romans. We cannot be sure their reports are true because they thought Celtic tribespeople were savages (wild and uncivilized). They probably did not understand Celtic culture either. Luckily, we also have archaeological finds that give us clues about the past.

▶ The Roman general Julius Caesar wrote that the Celtic peoples in Gaul sacrificed people to please their gods.

▲ The horned god Cernunnos was associated with the harvest.

OFFERINGS AND SACRIFICES

In Celtic cultures, people gave offerings to their gods. They left precious objects, such as shields, swords or jewels, in sacred places. They also sacrificed animals. Perhaps they did this to pray for a good harvest – or to say thank you for one. There is evidence that they sacrificed humans, too (see page 71).

◀ This Iron Age bronze shield was found in the River Thames near Wandsworth. Experts think it was thrown into the river as a gift to the gods.

Stories

Bran was a Welsh giant whose cauldron brought dead warriors back to life.

During the Iron Age, storytelling was the main entertainment. Stories were not written down until much later – they were simply passed on by word of mouth. Celtic **myths** and legends are part of the culture in Ireland, Wales, Scotland and Brittany. They are so powerful that people still enjoy them today.

COMMON CHARACTERS

Some characters crop up in many different stories, and these stories are grouped together as story cycles. The famous Ulster Cycle tells the adventures of the Irish warrior-king Cuchulain (say Koo-kull-in). The Fenian Cycle is all about a hero called Finn MacCool (see below left).

▲ In this illustration, Cuchulain is driven into battle in his chariot.

THE GIANT'S CAUSEWAY

In some stories, Finn MacCool is a giant. According to legend, he was responsible for the Giant's Causeway, a 'road' of rocks that leads from the coast of northern Ireland to the Scottish island of Staffa. Finn built it to go after a rival Scottish giant called Benandonner.

▶ In reality, the stones of the Giant's Causeway are columns of black volcanic rock that were formed more than 50 million years ago.

BLODEUWEDD

Welsh myths tell of Blodeuwedd (say blod-EYE-weth), a goddess made out of flowers. She was turned into an owl as punishment for betraying her husband.

FANTASTIC THEMES

Stories change a little each time they are told. However, when the Celtic myths were eventually written down, they probably contained similar ingredients to the stories told in earlier times. As well as brave heroes who overcome impossible odds, there are also enchanted beasts, spirits, fairies, giants and other supernatural beings, such as the Green Man.

▲ This storyteller is dressed to look like the Green Man – a mythical character who is linked to spring and regrowth, as well as to the Celtic god Cernunnos (see pages 66–67).

MAGIC CAULDRONS

Cauldrons were ritual objects for the druids. In Celtic myths, they often have the magical ability to help things grow back. There are stories about cooking pots that never run out of food, and even cauldrons that bring the dead back to life.

◀ This silver cauldron was probably made by Thracians, not Celtic peoples, but it shows Celtic characters and themes. One scene (top) shows a dead warrior being put into a magic cauldron.

Burying the dead

In Britain, the only Iron Age cemeteries that have been found are in what is now east Yorkshire. It seems that most people at this time did not bury their dead in ways that survive for us to find.

CREMATIONS

Most Iron Age Britons probably **cremated** their dead. Perhaps the custom was to scatter ashes, because very few sites with buried ashes have been found. One site was at Welwyn, in Hertfordshire. A decorated wooden bucket held the ashes, along with bronze jugs and a pan. A similar burial was uncovered at Aylesford in Kent.

CHARIOT BURIALS

Most of the bodies found in east Yorkshire had been buried with no grave goods, or just a few, but seven of the burials contained chariots. The most famous is at Wetwang, where the grave was that of a woman. Such a fine burial shows she must have been of very high rank.

◄ *This bronze face decorates the wooden bucket that was found at the Aylesford burial.*

▲ *These Iron Age grave goods were found in a grave in Welwyn, Hertfordshire.*

Bog people

Many hundreds of bodies of Iron Age people have been found in peat bogs. The conditions there – very acidic water and almost no oxygen – are perfect for preserving bodies. Some bog people died natural deaths, but many show signs that they were human sacrifices.

LINDOW MAN

Lindow Man was found in a peat bog in Cheshire, England, in 1984. He must have been from a rich family because his beard, moustache and nails were neatly trimmed. However, his throat was cut and he had been hit on the head. It looks as if he was killed to please the gods. His last meal was another clue that his death was part of a ritual – it included pollen from mistletoe, a plant sacred in Celtic religion.

▲ Like all bog people, Lindow Man's skin had been stained brown by the peat.

CLONYCAVAN MAN

Discovered in an Irish peat bog in 2003, Clonycavan Man died a violent death. Like Lindow Man, he was probably a man of high rank. His hair was styled with costly oil. Clonycavan Man died about 2300 years ago. Archaeologists believe he might have been a chief or king.

▼ Bog bodies may be found when peat is being harvested. The peat is used as fuel and for potting plants.

▼ Tollund Man, found in Denmark, is one of the best-preserved bog bodies. He died about 300 bce.

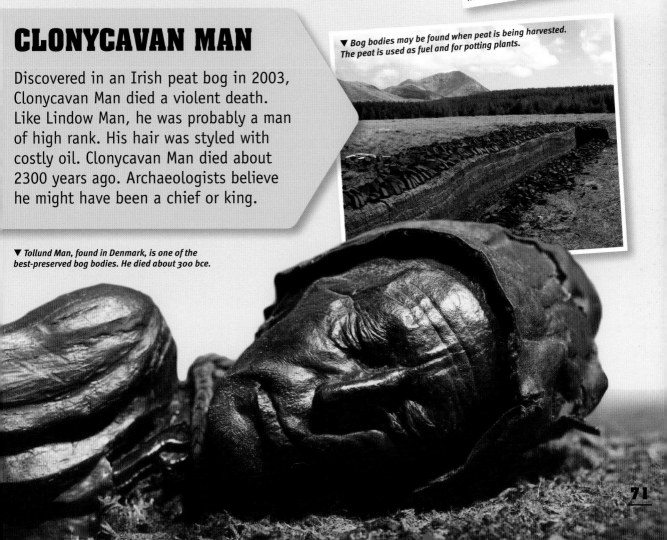

Celtic warriors

Roman writers describe Celtic peoples as warlike, constantly fighting with each other from their hill forts (see pages 58–59). As well as fights between rival tribes, the end of the Iron Age saw battles against the Romans.

WARRIORS

Men and women took part in the fighting. Most fought on foot, although some rode war chariots. They did not wear armour – in fact, the Romans claimed that Celtic warriors did not wear any clothes and went into battle naked!

WEAPONS

Iron Age warriors fought with iron swords and iron-tipped spears, and defended themselves with shields, which came in many different shapes. They also fired stones from slingshots, but do not appear to have used bows and arrows.

ROMAN INVASIONS

The Roman general Julius Caesar invaded Britain from northern Gaul in 55 BCE, but local warriors drove him off. He returned the next year with more troops, but still did not capture the island. When the Romans next tried, nearly one hundred years later, they had more success. General Aulus Plautius arrived in 43 CE, and took control of southeastern Britain. By 84 CE, most of England and Wales was part of the Roman **Empire**.

◀ *Extent of Roman Empire (black) in 84 ce.*

Boudicca's forces, from the Iceni and Trinovantes tribes, numbered about 100,000.

CARATACUS

Caratacus was a chief of the Catuvellauni tribe. He fought off the invading Roman force led by Aulus Plautius, but suffered defeats at the Battles of the Medway and the Thames, in southeastern England. He was then taken as a prisoner to Rome, and his stronghold, Colchester, became Britain's first Roman city.

Caratacus

▲ Caratacus fought off troops of Roman legionaries (foot soldiers) like these.

◀ Celtic warriors tattooed their bodies and painted themselves with woad (a blue natural plant dye) to appear more terrifying.

BOUDICCA

Boudicca was queen of the Iceni tribe of eastern England. When her husband died, the Romans quickly took control of his kingdom. Boudicca led a rebellion against the Romans, capturing and destroying the cities of Colchester, London and St Albans. She was eventually defeated at the Battle of Watling Street.

Statue of Boudicca

Roman Britain

The Roman invasion of Britain brought about the end of the Iron Age, and of prehistory. When the Romans arrived in Britain in 43 CE, they quickly occupied the southeastern corner of the island. Over the following decades, they conquered England, Wales and part of Scotland. 'Britannia' became a province of the Roman Empire. The occupation lasted until 409 CE.

▲ This beautiful mosaic decorates the floor of a Roman villa at Lullingstone, Kent. The villa probably belonged to Pertinax, Britannia's governor from 185 to 187 CE.

▼ The Romans built a coast-to-coast defensive wall, Hadrian's Wall, to protect Britannia from invasion from the north.

Built between 122 and 128 CE, Hadrian's Wall stretches 117.5 kilometres.

FINAL BATTLES

The Romans got as far north as they were going to by late summer 84 CE. This was when Agricola, then Roman governor of Britannia, defeated the Caledonian tribes. The battle took place at Mons Graupius, in the Scottish Highlands. After his victory, Agricola withdrew south again.

Governor Agricola

▲ *The Romans built more than 150 forts to defend their province. This one in London would have housed up to 1000 soldiers.*

OCCUPYING FORCE

The Romans built roads to link the towns in their new province. They also built forts for their soldiers, called legionaries. The legionaries crushed rebellions and defended important places, such as quarries or river crossings.

ROMAN CULTURE

The Romans brought their own way of life to Britain. As well as building towns, forts and roads, they introduced different gods, festivals and customs. Gradually the Britons adopted some of these new ways, and slowly the two cultures mixed together.

▼ *Many Roman buildings still stand today, including this bathhouse in Bath, southwest England.*

CELTIC CHRISTIANITY

The Romans never conquered the far north of Scotland or Ireland. However, Celtic peoples there would soon encounter a different new influence: Christianity. St Augustine arrived in Britain in the 500s CE to convert people to Christianity. The religion took hold, and the old Celtic beliefs died out.

Treasure hoards

Archaeologists have built up a picture of prehistoric Britain by looking at clues – bones, tools, weapons, buildings and treasure. Hoards of treasure may have been gifts to the gods, or simply belongings that were hidden to keep them safe. These are some of Britain's best prehistoric hoards:

HOARDS

A hoard is a collection of valuable objects – coins, jewellery or objects made from precious metals.

6 | *Isleham Hoard c. 1150–1000 bce*

▶ *This person is using a metal detector. It will beep if it senses metal underground – perhaps it will be an ancient treasure hoard!*

8 | *8) Stirling Hoard c. 300–100 bce*

9 | *Ipswich Hoard c. 75 bce*

PRECIOUS FINDS

Some hoards are found by treasure hunters using metal detectors. Others are uncovered accidentally by construction workers or farmers. Finders have to report their find to an official. If it counts as a hoard, it is offered for sale to a museum.

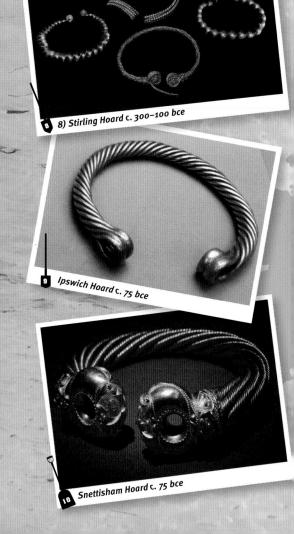
10 | *Snettisham Hoard c. 75 bce*

YORK HOARD
c. 3000 bce
This New Stone Age hoard was found in 1868 and included more than 70 flint tools.

AYTON EAST FIELD HOARD
c. 3000–2500 bce
This New Stone Age hoard was found in a burial cairn in North Yorkshire in 1848. It included flint axes, flint knives and boar-tusk blades.

MIGDALE HOARD
c. 2000 bce
This Early Bronze Age hoard included bronze bracelets, bronze anklets and carved jet buttons. Workmen found the hoard in the Scottish Highlands in 1900.

NEAR LEWES HOARD
c. 1400–1250 bce
This Middle Bronze Age hoard contains more than 50 objects. There are torcs, bracelets, gold discs and rings, as well as amber beads from the Baltic.

MILTON KEYNES HOARD
c. 1150–800 bce
This Late Bronze Age hoard was made up of a plain pottery bowl containing more than two kilograms of gold torcs and bracelets.

ISLEHAM HOARD
c. 1150–1000 bce
Discovered in Ely, Cambridgeshire, in 1959, this is England's largest Bronze Age hoard. It contained more than 6,500 bronze items.

COLLETTE HOARD
c. 1000–800 bce
This Bronze Age hoard was found in 2005 near Berwick-upon-Tweed, Northumberland. It included gold hair decorations, bracelets, rings and tools.

STIRLING HOARD
c. 300–100 bce
Discovered in Stirlingshire, Scotland, in 2009, this Iron Age hoard is made up of four gold torcs, one of which was broken.

IPSWICH HOARD
c. 75 bce
Construction workers found this Iron Age hoard in Suffolk in 1968. It included six spectacular gold torcs.

SNETTISHAM HOARD
c. 75 bce
This spectacular Iron Age torc was found in Norfolk in 1948. Further excavations in 1990 led to 75 more torcs being discovered.

WINCHESTER HOARD
c. 75–25 bce
This Iron Age hoard was found in a field in Hampshire in 2000. Its two torcs were made from a chain of looped gold rings, rather than the usual twisted thread.

LITTLE HORWOOD HOARD
c. 50 bce
Metal detectors found this Iron Age hoard of more than 70 staters (ancient coins) in 2006. It was probably part of the Whaddon Chase hoard.

WICKHAM MARKET HOARD
c. 25 bce–25 ce
This hoard of 840 Iron Age gold coins was discovered in Suffolk in 2008 with a metal detector. Almost all of the coins had been made by the Iceni tribe.

WHADDON CHASE HOARD
c. 0–100 ce
Farmworkers found this Iron Age hoard of staters (ancient coins) in 1849. There may have been as many as 2000 coins, but onlookers pocketed some of the treasure!

HALLATON TREASURE
c. 40s ce
A metal detector discovered this Iron Age hoard in 2000. It was made up of more than 5000 gold and silver coins, guarded by a real dog, and a Roman helmet.

SILSDEN HOARD
c. 50 ce
A metal detector found this Iron Age hoard in West Yorkshire in 1998. It consists of 27 gold coins and a Roman gemstone ring.

KEY FINDS

This map shows where some of the most important prehistoric treasure hoards were found.

◀ Hundreds of hoards have been discovered around Britain. This map just shows 16 of them.

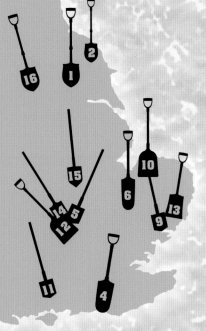

GLOSSARY

ARCHAEOLOGIST
Someone who studies the things that people from the past made and used, as a way of finding out how they lived.

BARROW
A large mound of earth or stones, often built to mark a burial site.

BEAKER CULTURE
Relating to a people in western and central Europe in the Copper Age, known for their bell-shaped pots.

CELTIC
Describes a culture and language shared by many tribes across Europe during the Iron Age.

CHALCOLITHIC
The Copper Age, when people were first working copper and gold. In Britain it lasted from about 2500 to 2200 BCE.

CREMATE
To burn a body after death.

DNA
A chemical made up of spiral molecules, found in living cells. It carries genes – the instructions for life.

DOLMEN
A New Stone Age monument (often set up to mark a person's grave) with a flat stone resting on two or more upright stones.

DOMESTICATE
To tame and keep a wild animal.

DRUID
A Celtic priest.

EMPIRE
A group of lands or peoples brought under the rule of one government or person.

EURASIA
A term used to describe the combined landmass of Europe and Asia.

EXCAVATE
To dig up.

FIRE DRILL
A tool made from a pointed stick and a flat piece of wood, used for lighting fires.

FLINT KNAPPER
Someone who makes tools by chipping away at flint, a type of hard stone.

GAULS
The Roman name for the people from Gallia, the region that is now France, Luxembourg and Belgium.

GLACIER
A huge, slow-moving sheet of ice.

GRAVE GOODS
Objects placed in a grave or tomb for use in the afterlife.

HILL FORT
A hilltop surrounded by defensive banks and ditches.

HUNTER-GATHERER
Someone who lives by hunting, fishing and collecting wild plant foods.

ICE AGE
A period when the climate is so cold that glaciers stretch out from the poles.

MESOLITHIC
The Middle Stone Age, when people were hunter-gatherers and used advanced stone tools. In Britain the Middle Stone Age lasted from about 11,500 to 6000 years ago.

MYTH
An old story that contains ideas about ancient times or supernatural beings.

NEOLITHIC
The New Stone Age, when people shifted from hunter-gathering to farming, still using stone tools.
In Britain, the New Stone Age lasted from about 4000 to 2500 BCE.

PALAEOLITHIC
The Old Stone Age, when people were hunter-gatherers and used simple tools of stone, wood and bone. In Britain the Old Stone Age lasted from about 900,000 to 11,500 years ago.

PASSAGE GRAVE
A tomb at the end of a stone passage, buried under an earth mound.

PEAT BOG
An area of wet, spongy ground where acidic conditions stop plants (and human bodies) from rotting properly.

PREDATOR
An animal that hunts and eats other animals for food.

PULSES
Vegetable plants, such as peas, beans and lentils, grown for their seeds.

QUARRY
An open place where stone is cut out of the ground.

ROMANS
People from Ancient Rome, a civilization that flourished across Europe, Asia and north Africa (at its height about 117 CE).

SACRIFICES
Things of value given up – or an animal or person who was killed – often as an offering to please a god.

SOLSTICE
Midsummer or midwinter. In the northern half of the world, these fall on 21 June and 22 December.

WATTLE AND DAUB
Wattle means strips of wood, and daub is a sticky mix of clay, straw and dung.

INDEX

Picture credits (t=top, b=bottom, l=left, r=right, c=centre, fc=front cover)
Maps: Philip Schwartzberg Meridian Mapping 6/7, 17, 44bl, 55.
Illustrations: Laszlo Veres, Beehive 10, 18, 22/23, 32cr, 39t, 42/43, 58/59; Sam Weston, Linden Artists 45, 60.
Photographs (© the photographers)
Alamy 12/13 © Heritage Image Partnership Ltd, 13tr © The Art Archive, 14cl © World History Archive, 15 (main) © Jose A Astor, 16tr © Jeff Morgan 16, 19 (main) © Clearview, 21tl © David Wall, 27 (main) © MS Bretherton, 30br © Skyscan Photolibrary, 32cl © Heritage Image Partnership Ltd, 35cr © A.P.S. (UK), 37 (main) © Terry Mathews, 40tr © Chris Howes/Wild Places Photography, 41br © World History Archive, 43tr a)© Nigel Spooner, 43tr b)© Nearby, 44 (main) © David McGill, 46/47 © Terry Mathews, 48 (main) © lowefoto, 50br © Dave Porter, 50/51 © imagebroker, 52 (main) © lowefoto, 53 (main) © CountrySideCollection - Homer Sykes, 53bl © Anglia Images, 54tr © Heritage Image Partnership Ltd, 55tr © Heritage Image Partnership Ltd, 58tr © Commission Air, 58cl © Heritage Image Partnership Ltd, 61cl © North Wind Picture Archives, 62 (main) © Powered by Light/Alan Spencer, 62bl © Jacqui Hurst, 65tr © Ilan Amihai, 66/67 (main) © Heritage Image Partnership Ltd, 68tr © Heritage Image Partnership Ltd, 68/69 © Mark Bourdillon, 69tr © Matthew Taylor, 69cr © Heritage Image Partnership Ltd, 69bl © The Print Collector, 70 (main) © Heritage Image Partnership Ltd, 70bl © Peter Horree, 76 b) © sandy young. © **Archaeology South-East, UCL** 27tr. **Corbis Images** 8 (main) © Arthur Dorety/Stocktrek Images, 9 (main) © Leonello Calvetti/Stocktrek Images, 11bl © A9999 Juraj Liptak/dpa, 14cb © Visuals Unlimited, 19bl © Sorokin Donat/ITAR-TASS Photo, 30cl © Alun Bull/English Heritage/Arcaid, 32br © Adam Woolfitt, 35 (main) © Craig Joiner/Loop Images, 36 (main) © Chris Hill/National Geographic Creative, 36br © Gianni Dagli Orti, 43bl © Steven Vidler, 46cr © Last Refuge/Robert Harding World Imagery, 46br © Last Refuge/Robert Harding World Imagery, 49 (main) © Last Refuge/Robert Harding World Imagery, 54bl © Walter Geiersperger, 54bl © Walter Geiersperger, 55bl © Heritage Images, 56l © Christophe Boisvieux, 59bc © Skyscan, 60br b) © Fritz, Albert/The food passionates, 64cl © Werner Forman/Werner Forman, 64/65 © Werner Forman/Werner Forman, 65tl © Steven Vidler, 67tr © Heritage Images, 67bc © Werner Forman/Werner Forman, 71b © Christophe Boisvieux, 74tr © Jonathan Bailey/English Heritage/Arcaid, 74/75 © Craig Easton/cultura, 75tl © Heritage Images. **Fotolibra** 25tl Mark Gregor Ferguson, 25cr Mark Gregor Ferguson, 31t Miles Kelly Publishing, 60cr Miles Kelly Publishing. **Getty Images** 10br Print Collector / Contributor, 11tr AFP / Stringer, 14tr Dea Picture Library / Contributor, 16br AJ Wilhelm, 21 (main) Danita Delimont, 23cr Eric Cabanis/AFP/Getty Images, 28/29 (main) Jim Richardson, 29tr Print Collector / Contributor, 30bl Print Collector / Contributor, 33tr Paul HANNY / Contributor, 33bl (figure) AFP / Stringer, 38tr Image Hans Elbers, 38/39 (main) Nikki Bidgood, 41tr Print Collector / Contributor, 44tr Steve Gorton, 49bl Sebastian Willnow/Staff, 51bl Matt Cardy / Stringer, 59cr Last Refuge, 60br a) Photofusion / Contributor, 61br Print Collector / Contributor, 63br Colin Weston, 65bc Print Collector / Contributor, 71tr Print Collector / Contributor, 73tl Neil Holmes, 73tr Hulton Archive / Handout, 74br De Agostini / W. Buss. © **Historic England** 12cl. © **James Dilley - Ancient Craft** 18c. © **Dr Jocelyne Dudding, Museum of Archaeology and Anthropology, Cambridge** 22cr. © **Peterborough Museum and Art Gallery - Vivacity** 52cr. **Photoshot** 76 c) © World History Archive/Photoshot. © **Portable Antiquities Scheme** (CC by attribution licence) 6tr, 19cr **Science Photo Library** 4tr Richard Bizley, 5 Richard Bizley, 7cr Natural History Museum, London, 7br Science Picture Co, 13bl David Gifford, 15cl Dirk Wiersma, 15bc Javier Trueba/MSF, 26 (main) Jose Antonio Peñas. **Shutterstock.com** All fc photos, 2bl Robert Adrian Hillman, 2/3b Tetiana Dziubanovska, 2/3t vladimir salman, 4br Designua, 8bl Incredible Arctic, 9br oorka, 10cr Stacey Newman, 11 (main) Villy Yovcheva, 13br ErickN, 20 (main) Matt Gibson, 20br Holly Kuchera, 24 BasPhoto, 25 (map) Volina, 25bl Edward Haylan, 25br jaroslava V, 31br JKtu_21, 33 b/g Eder, 34 Kwiatek7, 36cl UnaPhoto, 37br Stephane Bidouze, 41 (map) Volina, 42tr a) Jiri Vaclavek, 42tr b) pixelman, 45cr vectorOK, 49tl jennyt, 50tr dashadima, 55br Boris Stroujko, 56 b/g katatonia82, 56cr (frame) gillmar, 57 (map) dashadima, 57tr Renata Sedmakova, 63 (main) Andrew McLean, 64tr a) art_of_sun, 64tr b) Peter Hermes Furian, 67tl T.Fabian, 68br Koshevnyk, 71c Michael Steden, 71 b/g vladimir salman, 72/73 b/g Shaiith, 72/73 (warrior) Stamatoyoshi, 73br maziarz, 74br (frame) gillmar, 75cr joeborg, 75bl Morphart Creation, 76 (main) Martin Christopher Parker, 76d) Jason Benz Bennee, 77 (map) dashadima. © **South West Maritime Archaeological Group (SWMAG)** 50cl, 50cr. © **St Edmundsbury Heritage Service** 40bl, 76 a). © **Wessex Archaeology** 45tr, 45br. **Wiki Commons** (Creative Commons 3.0 Unported Generic Licence/Creative Commons Attribution-Share Alike 3.0 Unported) 26tr Wolfgang Sauber, 26br Yelkrokoyade, 33br Bullenwächter, 39cl Joseph Lertola (public domain), 47tl public domain, 48bl Midnightblueowl, 56cr Med.